Office 2000
Made Simple

P.K.McBride

**MADE SIMPLE
BOOKS**

OXFORD AUCKLAND BOSTON JOHANNESBURG MELBOURNE NEW DELHI

Made Simple
An imprint of Butterworth-Heinemann
Linacre House, Jordan Hill, Oxford OX2 8DP
225 Wildwood Avenue, Woburn MA 01801-2041
A division of Reed Educational and Professional Publishing Ltd

ℝ   A member of the Reed Elsevier plc group

First published 2000
© P K McBride 2000

TRADEMARKS/REGISTERED TRADEMARKS
Computer hardware and software brand names mentioned in this book are protected
by their respective trademarks and are acknowledged.

British Library Cataloguing in Publication Data
A catalogue record for this book is available from the British Library.

ISBN 0 7506 4179 7

⚒ Typeset by Elle and P.K.McBride, Southampton
Icons designed by Sarah Ward © 1994
Printed and bound in Great Britain

Contents

Preface

This book is intended to be a companion to those others in this series that focus on individual applications in the Office suite. *Office 2000 Made Simple* provides a brief introduction to the three main packages, Word, Excel and PowerPoint, and a more detailed coverage of:

- the Office environment;
- those features and ways of working that are common to the applications;
- transferring and sharing data between applications, through copying, linking and Binders;
- the graphing and graphical add-ons that can be used within all applications;
- Outlook, Office 2000's personal organiser;
- integration with the Internet, through e-mail and World Wide Web links.

The Office 2000 suite contains so much, that it is not possible to cover it all in a book this size. I hope that I have included enough, and in enough detail, to give you what you need to get started and to work effectively across the applications.

To find out more about the individual components, see:

Access 2000 Made Simple by Moira Stephen
Excel 2000 Made Simple by Stephen Morris
FrontPage 2000 Made Simple by Nat McBride
Internet Explorer 5 Made Simple by P.K. McBride
Outlook 2000 Made Simple by P.K. McBride
PowerPoint 2000 Made Simple by Moira Stephen
Publisher 2000 Made Simple by Moira Stephen
Word 2000 Made Simple by Keith Brindley

Take note

Access, Excel and Word 2000 Made Simple are published in both regular and business editions.

1 Office management

The Office equipment

In the last few years Microsoft Office has established itself as the leading business application software suite. Office 2000, the latest version, has been rewritten to give better integration between the components, and simple access to the Internet.

The Office 2000 suite comes in several editions. All contain:

Word – a word processor that is easy to use at a basic level, yet has most of the features of a DTP package;

Excel – a spreadsheet that is powerful enough to handle the accounts of a multi-million pound company, yet simple enough for a child to use for a school project;

Outlook is a comprehensive organiser, serving as a diary, job planner, address book, mail centre and more;

Binder – a leap forward in integration, allowing you to store different application documents in one file, and to switch easily between them.

Depending upon the edition, you may also have:

Access – a richly featured and highly powerful database management system;

PowerPoint – presentation software, for producing slideshows and accompanying handouts and notes;

FrontPage – for creating professional Web pages and managing Web sites;

Publisher – desktop publishing software;

Small Business Customer Manager, and …

Small Business Financial Manager, integrated tools for businesses.

The hardware

Minimum requirements

Processor Pentium 75MHz

RAM　　32 Mb (95/98)
　　　　48 Mb (NT)

Hard disk 250 Mb free

Monitor　VGA 800 × 640

❑ And these are the bare minimums. For decent performance, or if you are using PhotoDraw, then double all the figures – the hardware ought to be worth more than the software!

Take note

This book concentrates on the common features and core applications.

Minor applications

Office 2000 has a large set of minor applications that are mainly run from within a major program. These include:

- software to add clip art, graphs, equations, charts, and decorative text to Word or Powerpoint documents;

- converters to read files from other word-processors, spreadsheets and databases into Office applications, and to save files in formats suitable for other systems;

- graphics filters to handle many different formats;

- DataMap to display regional data from Excel and Access on maps;

- System Info to analyse your computer system.

Running from hard disk or CD

Office applications are huge, but they don't have to swamp your hard disk. Many of the optional features and less commonly-used components can be run from the CDs, or installed from the CDs if and when they are needed (see the next page). It means that you will have to keep them in the drive, or at least close at hand, and that things will slow down when you need the extra functions, but it will cut down the hard disk requirements.

Take note

The Office package has an excellent Help system, with an Office Assistant that understands (more or less) plain English.

Tip

If you are short of disk space, a second hard drive can be installed cheaply and easily.

Installation

Office 2000 has a very efficient and easy-to-use installation routine. It will normally start automatically when you insert the CD – if it doesn't, use My Computer or Windows Explorer to open the CD drive and click **setup.exe** to set it going.

You have two choices:

● **Install Now** will perform a standard installation, putting the core files and a selection of components onto your hard disk. This is the best choice for people who are new to Microsoft Office.

● **Customize…** lets you select which components to install and where. Most applications have one or more levels of features – you can set the installation options either for the whole set or for individual features. If you have already used Office 2000 (or an earlier version) you should have an idea of what you do or don't need.

1 Put the CD in the drive and run Setup.

2 Enter your details and the CD-Key number.

3 Click Install Now.

Or

4 Click Customize…

5 Set the drive or folder then click Next>>.

6 Click ⊞ to display the features of an item.

7 Click 🖳▾ and select from the menu to change the installation option.

8 When you have worked through the set, click Install Now.

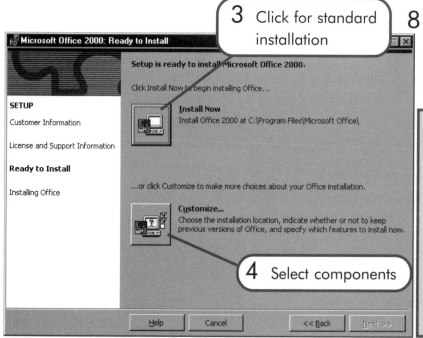

3 Click for standard installation

4 Select components

Take note

You can change your installation options at any later time through the Control Panel's Add/Remove Programs utility.

4

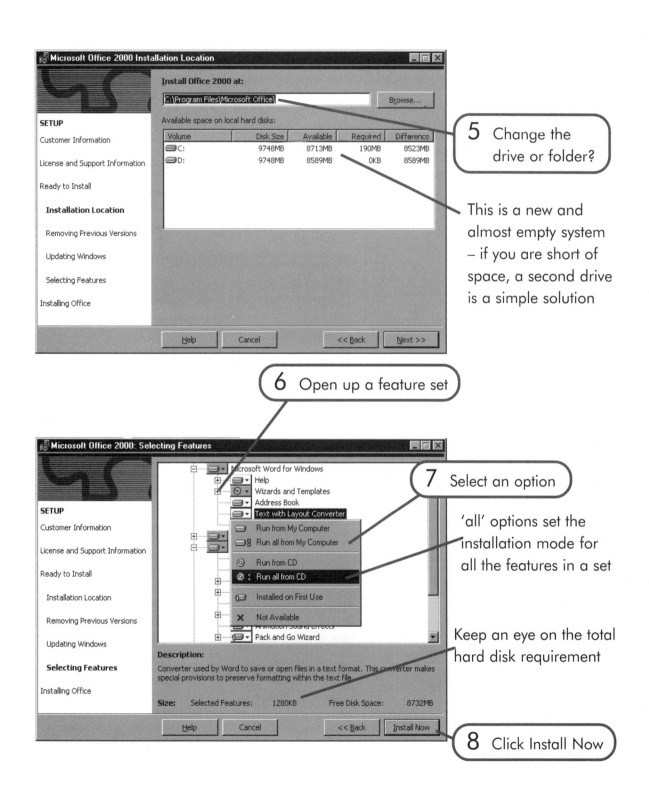

Microsoft Office 2000 Installation Location

Install Office 2000 at:

C:\Program Files\Microsoft Office\   Browse...

Available space on local hard disks:

Volume	Disk Size	Available	Required	Difference
C:	9748MB	8713MB	190MB	8523MB
D:	9748MB	8589MB	0KB	8589MB

SETUP

Customer Information

License and Support Information

Ready to Install

Installation Location

Removing Previous Versions

Updating Windows

Selecting Features

Installing Office

Help   Cancel   << Back   Next >>

5 Change the drive or folder?

This is a new and almost empty system – if you are short of space, a second drive is a simple solution

6 Open up a feature set

Microsoft Office 2000: Selecting Features

Microsoft Word for Windows
Help
Wizards and Templates
Address Book
Text with Layout Converter

Run from My Computer
Run all from My Computer
Run from CD
Run all from CD
Installed on First Use
Not Available
Pack and Go Wizard

SETUP

Customer Information

License and Support Information

Ready to Install

Installation Location

Removing Previous Versions

Updating Windows

Selecting Features

Installing Office

Description:
Converter used by Word to save or open files in a text format. This converter makes special provisions to preserve formatting within the text file.

Size: Selected Features: 1280KB   Free Disk Space: 8732MB

Help   Cancel   << Back   Install Now

7 Select an option

'all' options set the installation mode for all the features in a set

Keep an eye on the total hard disk requirement

8 Click Install Now

5

Starting work

There are several ways to start Office applications – use the ones which work best for you.

The Start menu

You can start any application from the Start menu – they will all have been addded to it at installation. In fact, they will all have been thrown into the Programs group and this may make the menu too complicated – mine was very simple before!

Use the **Advanced** option on **Start – Settings – Taskbar & Start menu** to reorganise your Start menu to suit yourself. I've moved the shortcuts into a separate Office menu folder, with just Word, which I use most often, on the main Programs menu.

New and Open Documents can be moved off the main menu if you prefer

The Advanced option opens the Start menu in Explorer. Create a new folder if you want a new menu group, and drag shortcuts to reorganise the menu

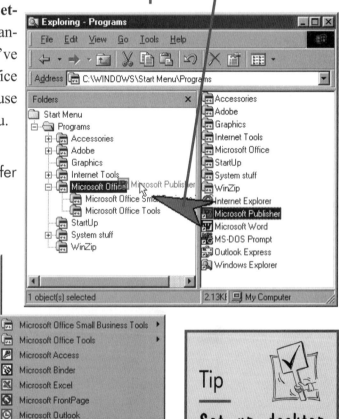

If you use an application a lot, keep a shortcut handy.

Tip

Set up desktop shortcuts to those applications that you use most often.

6

Starting from documents

The **New** and **Open Office Document** shortcuts – initially on the main menu – offer quick ways to start work on a file. This approach is good where you are mainly working on one document, rather than on a number within one application.

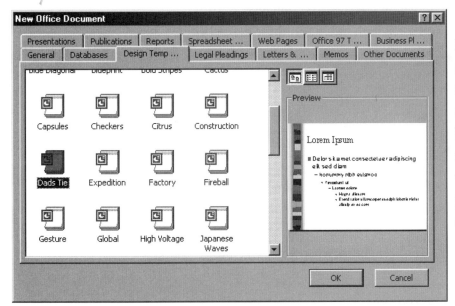

For a new document, switch to the tab, then select a template, wizard (see page 23) or blank document of the right type. The preview pane will give you an idea of the style and layout.

On the Open Document panel, you can find your recently used Office files in the History view. Just click on the name to open the document in its application.

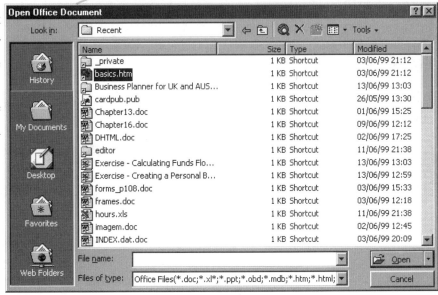

7

The Office Shortcut bar

The Office Shortcut bar comes equipped with buttons for opening or creating new Office files, adding tasks, contacts or appointments. You can also add shortcuts to Office (and other) applications.

When you first open the bar, you will be asked if you want it to open automatically on startup. Click 'Yes' if you do.

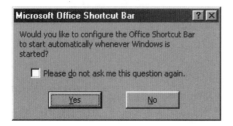

The shape and position the bar can be changed to suit your way of working. The bar can be a strip along any edge of the screen, or a floating strip or block. On an edge, it can be set to Auto Hide so that it disappears after use, and reappears when you point into that edge.

❑ Moving the Toolbar

1 Point to an empty part of the bar.

2 Drag to wherever you want it on the screen – to place it at an edge, push it slightly over.

❑ Adjusting the shape

3 Point to a side, to get the double-arrow cursor.

4 Drag to resize.

❑ Setting Auto Hide

5 Click the square at the top left of the Toolbar to open the menu.

6 Click to turn Auto Hide on ✓ or off.

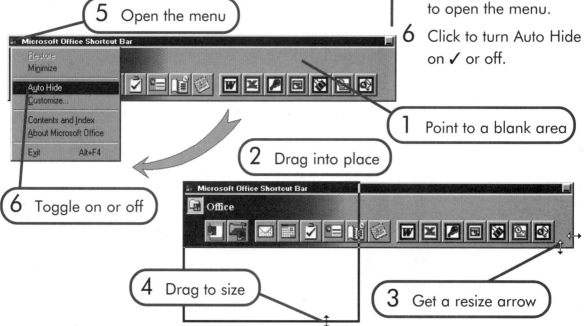

5 Open the menu

1 Point to a blank area

2 Drag into place

6 Toggle on or off

4 Drag to size

3 Get a resize arrow

Basic steps

1 Right click on the toolbar to open the short menu.

2 Select Customize.

3 Open the Buttons panel.

4 Pick a Toolbar.

5 Click the ☐ to add ✓ or remove a button.

6 Click ⬚ OK ⬚.

Customising the Shortcut bar

The most useful changes you can make to the Shortcut toolbar are to add to it buttons for the applications that you use – and remove unused ones. But you can also tailor its appearance, and you should check the **Settings** tab as this tells Office where to look for Templates (see page 23).

● As well as adding shortcuts from the Office set, you can also add a link to any other program on your system, or to a folder.

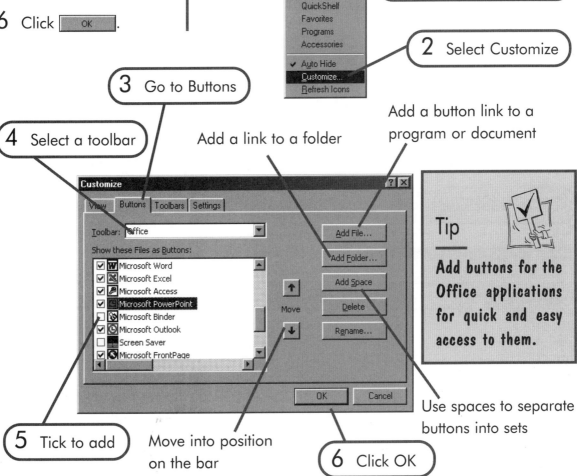

9

Multiple bars

An Office toolbar represents a folder. Its shortcuts, programs and sub-folders become items on the bar.

If you like the toolbar approach, you can create your own folder of shortcuts to favourite programs and make that into a toolbar.

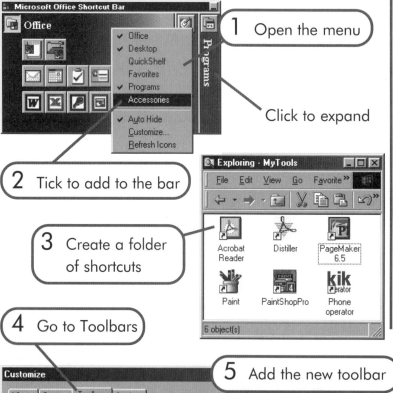

1 Open the menu

Click to expand

2 Tick to add to the bar

3 Create a folder of shortcuts

4 Go to Toolbars

5 Add the new toolbar

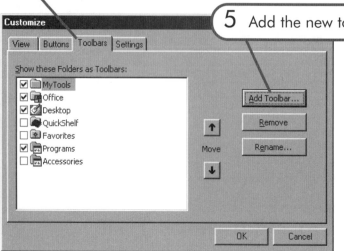

❏ Adding Toolbars

1 Right-click in a clear part of the Toolbar, to get the short menu.

2 Click on the name to add a toolbar.

❏ Creating toolbars

3 In Explorer, create a new folder and store in it shortcuts to your selected programs.

4 Open the Customize panel from the short menu and select Toolbars.

5 Click Add Toolbar and browse for the new shortcut folder.

Take note

You can only see the buttons of one toolbar at a time. Click on a compressed bar to open it up.

Basic steps

1 Right-click on the Toolbar to open the short menu.

2 Select Customize.

3 Open the View panel.

4 In the Colors pane, select the Toolbar then pick the Color and Fill style.

5 Try out any Options that seem worthwhile – you can always reset them again.

6 Click [OK].

Changing views

You can change the colour, button size and other aspects of the Toolbar displays, using the View panel.

The Options apply to all toolbars, though the Colour choices only apply to the selected toolbar.

These make Toolbars easier to use

3 Open the View panel

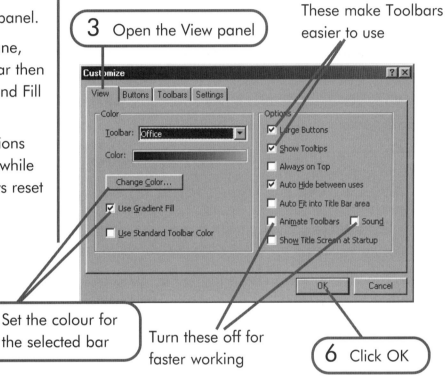

4 Set the colour for the selected bar

Turn these off for faster working

6 Click OK

Tip

If you want to use the Auto Hide feature, you may find it best to locate the Toolbar on the left edge of the screen. You are less likely to activate anything in it accidentally there than at the right or bottom (close to the scroll bars) or at the top (close to the menu bar and control buttons).

Summary

❑ The Office 2000 suite contains a set of major applications, plus many utilities that can be used from within the main applications.

❑ Installation is simple, and can be largely left to the Setup program, though there is a Customize option for people who have used Office software before, and know what components they want to install – and where to store them.

❑ The applications and their many optional features can be added or removed at any time.

❑ Office programs can be run from the Start menu, Desktop shortcuts or the Shortcut Bar – pick the approach that best suits your way of working.

❑ The Shortcut Bar can be placed anywhere on the screen, and can be set to hide itself when not in use.

❑ You can add buttons to the Shortcut Bar, and link other toolbars onto it.

2 Common features

Menus

The Office 2000 suite is huge and complex, but straightforward to use – at a basic level. (Mastery takes time!) A key factor in this ease of use is that – wherever possible – the same jobs are performed using the same buttons or menus. As there is a large core of common tasks, once you have got the hang of one application, you are on the way to learning the next.

Menus

Commands are grouped on menus, with only the more commonly-used ones visible at first. Browse through them to see the type of command to be found on each menu.

● An arrow to the right of an item leads to a sub-menu;

● If a menu item is followed by ... then selecting it opens up a dialog box where you specify details.

● If there is a ▭▼▭ at the bottom, clicking on it – or waiting a few seconds – will open up the full menu.

If you use a 'hidden' command, it will be displayed on the menu for the rest of the working session. If you use the same 'hidden' command regularly, it will be added to the visible set.

❑ Mouse control

1 Click on a name to open a menu.

2 Point to an arrowed item to open its menu.

3 Click on a menu item to select it.

❑ Keyboard control

4 Hold [Alt] and press the underlined letter to open a menu, then press an underlined letter to open a sub-menu or select a command, e.g. [Alt] + [I] then [P] then [H] selects Insert – Picture – Chart.

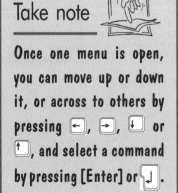

Click for the full menu

Take note

Once one menu is open, you can move up or down it, or across to others by pressing ⬅, ➡, ⬇ or ⬆, and select a command by pressing [Enter] or ⏎.

Context menus

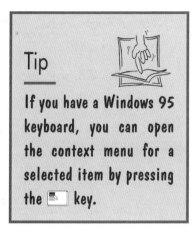
Like all software written to the Windows 95/98 standard, the Office applications produce context menus. These are opened by right-clicking on an item – a picture, cell, block of text, the page background or whatever – and display a selection of commands that may be used with that item.

The context menu for a block of text in Word – this one draws applicable commands from the Edit, Format and Insert menus

Dialog boxes

If a menu command is followed by ..., clicking on it will open a dialog box. These are used where there are range of options or where the command needs you to enter additional information.

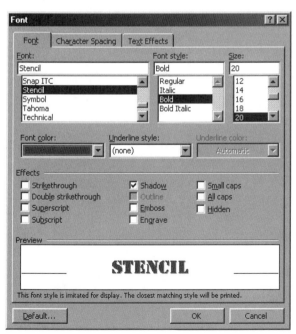

Many dialog boxes have several panels or tabs. Switch between them by clicking on the name at the top of the tab.

When you have finished with a dialog box, click **OK** to fix the selections or any entered data and close the box, or **Cancel** to abandon the changes and close.

Some dialog boxes also have an **Apply** button. Click this to apply the changes immediately without closing the box.

Custom menus

You may not want to customise menus straight away, but it is useful to know that it can be done. For instance, a *Close All* command might be useful if you regularly work with several documents open. You can add commands from any category onto any menu, though it helps to keep the same kind together.

Tip

To remove an command drag it from the menu and drop it into the Customize box.

Basic steps

1 On the Tools menu, select Customize...

2 Open the Commands panel.

3 Click on the menu to open it for editing.

4 Select a Category.

5 Find the Command that you want to add.

6 Drag it onto the menu.

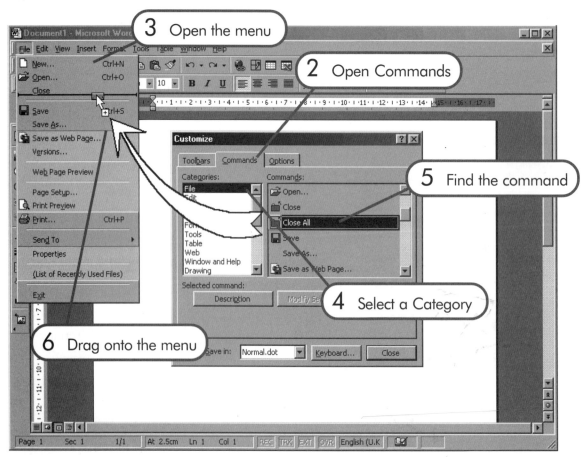

Basic steps

1 Open the Customize Commands panel from the Tools menu.

2 Select the menu item.

3 Click Modify Selection.

4 Point to Change Button Image and click on one to select it.

5 Click Close.

Menu item style

The Modify Selection option on the Customize box allows you to change the image, selection letter, grouping and other aspects of the appearance of menu items. Try changing the image – a good icon can help you find a command faster.

● You can only add images to simple commands – not to those that open submenus, or to those that are normally hidden.

● You can also change the [Alt] selection letter – indicated by '&' before it. To set a new selection letter, type '&' before it, and delete the existing '&'.

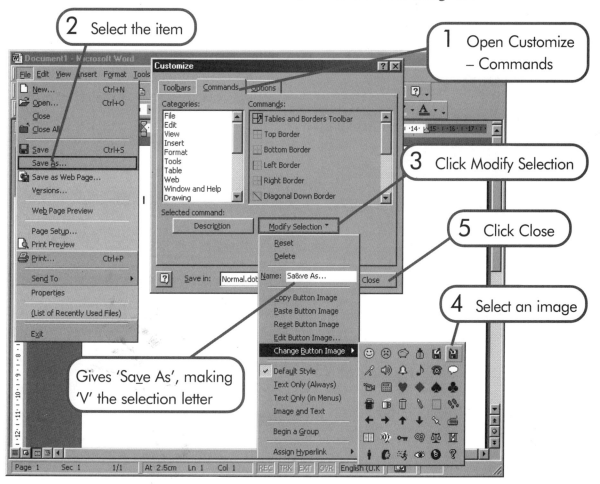

Toolbars

The buttons on the toolbars give quick and easy access to the more commonly-used commands. Each application has half a dozen or more toolbars, many of which – with variations – are found in all.

Some toolbars are open by default, but all can be displayed or removed as required. You can also add or remove buttons from any bar, see the next page.

Take note

The toolbars' titles are taken off if you merge the bars into the window frame (see page 29).

The Standard toolbars from Word (top), Excel (middle) and PowerPoint (bottom), hold the buttons for most commonly-used commands. Those for file handling, printing, editing, Internet access, zoom (screen magnification) and Help are present on all three toolbars.

Word, Excel and PowerPoint have these, though their contents vary slightly.

Formatting sets the style, alignment and layout of text.

Drawing has line and shape tools for creating diagrams.

Picture lets you control the appearance of an inserted picture.

Web turns the application into a Web browser for surfing the Internet.

Basic steps

Selecting toolbars

- ❏ Selecting toolbars

1 Open the View menu and select Toolbars...

Or

2 Right-click on any toolbar to open the same Toolbars menu.

3 Click a name to turn its display on ☑ or off.

- ❏ Customizing

4 From the Toolbars menu, pick Customize.

5 On the Options panel, adjust the display to suit yourself.

If you find toolbars useful – and you will – you can have more on screen than just the default ones. But don't overdo it. Every toolbar you add reduces the amount of visible working space!

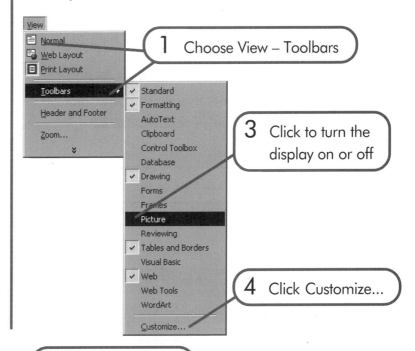

1 Choose View – Toolbars

3 Click to turn the display on or off

4 Click Customize...

A few toolbars are not on the Toolbars menu, but all are in the Toolbars panel – add or remove any from here.

ScreenTips remind you what the buttons do

Do you like to use keyboard shortcuts?

Animation is a pain in the eyes – ignore it

5 Adjust the display

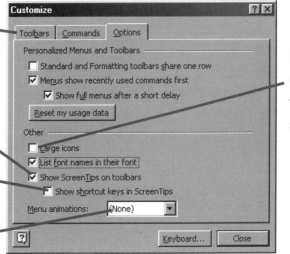

Large buttons are easier to see, but take up far more space

Placing toolbars

Button toolbars can be merged into the window frame, or allowed to 'float' on the document area. The position and size of floating toolbars can be adjusted at any time.

● Those bars that you want to use all of the time are probably best fitted into the frame.

● Those that are only wanted for the occasional job – e.g. *Drawing* for creating an illustration – can be brought up as needed, and floated in a convenient place.

Basic steps

1 Point to the title bar or to the lines at the start of the toolbar.

2 Drag the toolbar, pushing it off the edge if you want to merge it into the frame.

3 Release the mouse button.

4 Drag on an edge or corner to resize a floating toolbar.

Click the arrow to see the tool's options

You can drag bars within the frame, if needed

1 Point to the title bar or the lines

2 Drag the toolbar

3 Drop into place

4 Drag to adjust the size

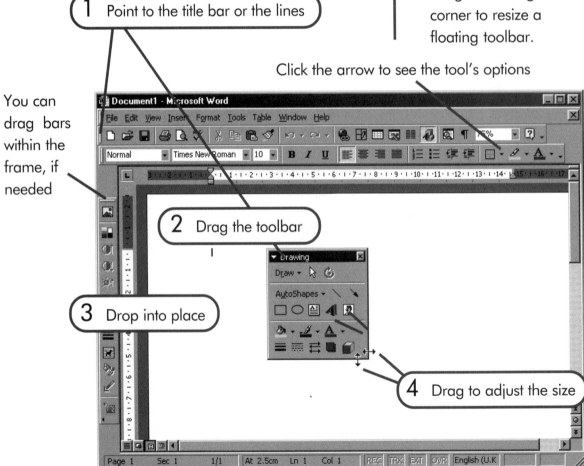

Basic steps

Adding and removing buttons

1 Click the little arrow-head at the end of a toolbar in the frame.

Or

2 Click the white arrow-head on a floating toolbar's title bar.

3 Click Add or Remove Buttons.

4 Click on a button name to turn it on or off.

5 Click anywhere else to close the list.

Every toolbar has an Add or Remove Buttons command which will display the full set of buttons for that toolbar. A simple click will then add or remove a button from the toolbar.

At some point, spend a few minutes adjusting the toolbars so that you have easy access to the tools you use most, without the clutter of rarely-used tools.

Take note

You can also add or remove toolbar buttons using the Customize tab — just drag them onto the toolbar instead of a menu.

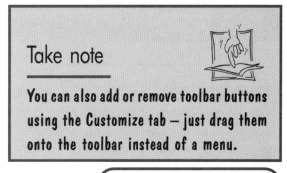

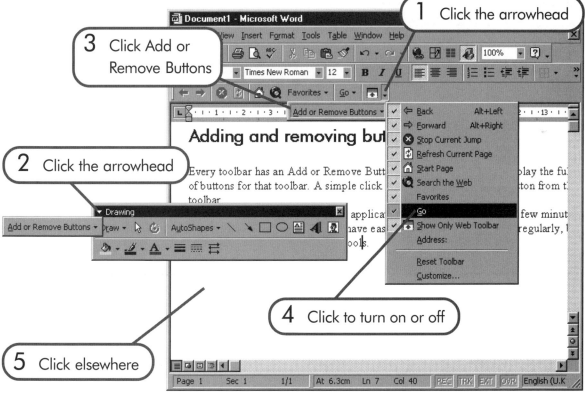

1 Click the arrowhead

3 Click Add or Remove Buttons

2 Click the arrowhead

4 Click to turn on or off

5 Click elsewhere

New documents

You can start a new document from the Office Shortcut bar as well as from within applications. The document can be based on a 'blank', or on a template or wizard. These can both help you to create attractive, effective documents, spreadsheets and presentations, but approach them from different ways.

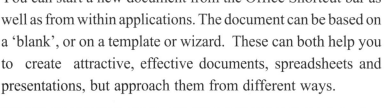

1 Click New Document

2 Use File – New

If you upgraded from Office 97, its templates will be here

The Previews are small but useful

3 Open a panel

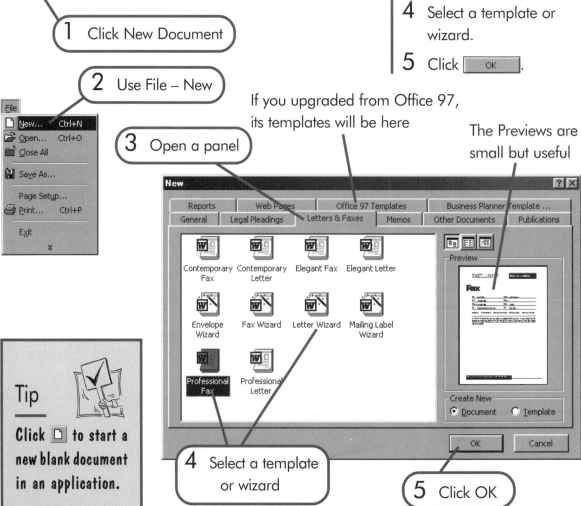

Tip

Click ▢ to start a new blank document in an application.

4 Select a template or wizard

5 Click OK

Templates and wizards

Fonts, styles and layouts are already in place

Templates are designed and formatted layouts with 'Click here to enter...' prompts wherever your own data is needed; Excel templates also have appropriate headings and formulae.

Some templates have macros (interactive mini-programs) to help you customize the document

Insert or replace text where indicated

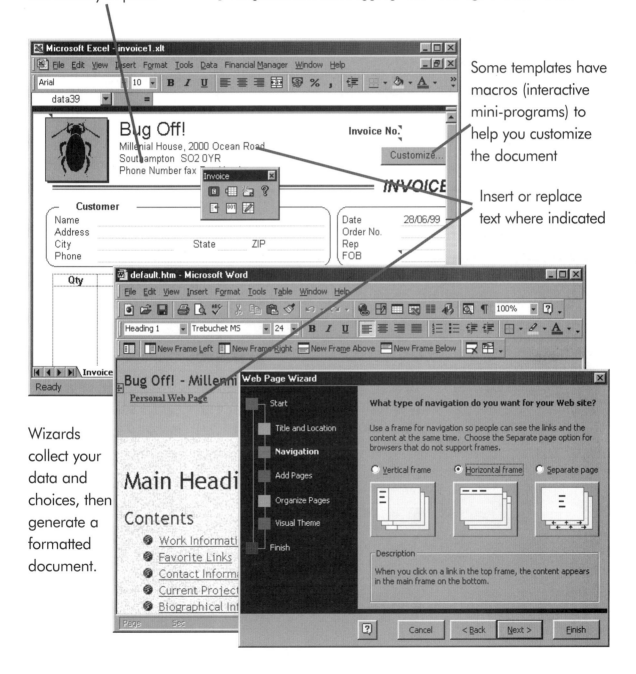

Wizards collect your data and choices, then generate a formatted document.

Opening files

There are several ways to open an existing Office file. Which way to take depends largely upon where you are when you start:

● If you have not yet opened the application, use Open on the Office Shortcut bar or select Open Office Document from the Start menu.

● If the application is open, and you want an old file, use the File Open command or the ☞ button.

● If the application is open and the file has been used recently, open the File menu and select it from the set at the bottom of the menu.

❏ From Windows

1 Click 🖳 on the Shortcut bar.

Or

2 Click Start and select Open Office Document.

❏ From an application

3 Click ☞ on the standard Toolbar.

Or

4 Open the File menu and select Open.

5 Choose a Look in area – e.g. *History* or *My Documents*.

6 Open the folder if necessary.

7 Set the Files of type to the appropriate type.

8 If you want details of the files, click 🖩▾ and select the Preview or Properties view.

9 Select the file and click ☞ Open .

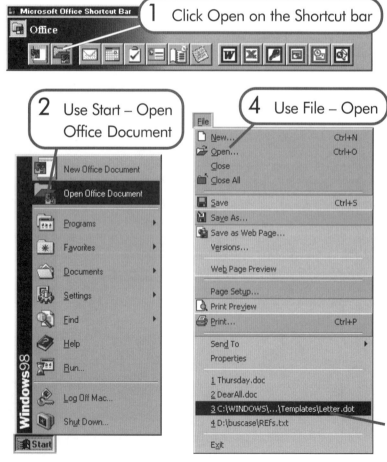

1 Click Open on the Shortcut bar

2 Use Start – Open Office Document

4 Use File – Open

Select a recently used file from the bottom of the File menu

24

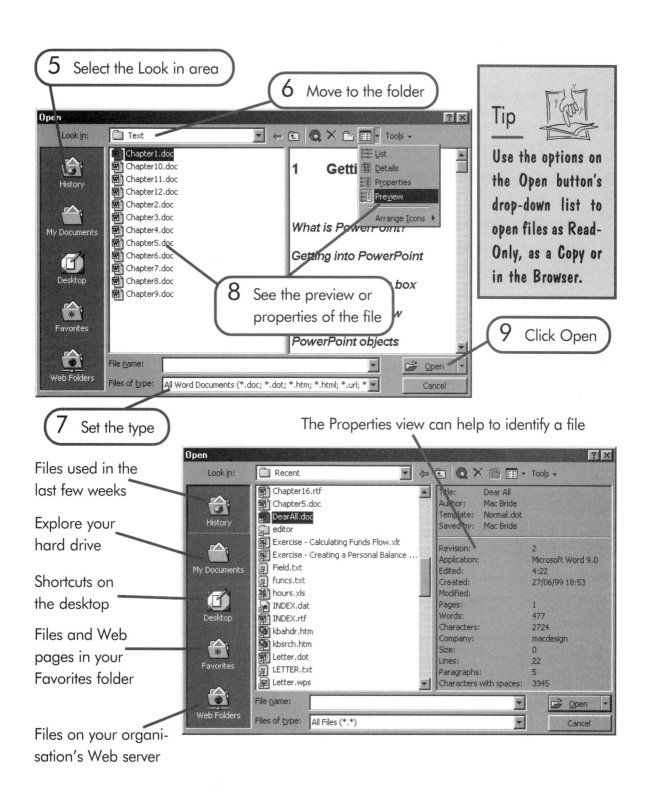

5 Select the Look in area

6 Move to the folder

8 See the preview or properties of the file

9 Click Open

7 Set the type

Tip

Use the options on the Open button's drop-down list to open files as Read-Only, as a Copy or in the Browser.

The Properties view can help to identify a file

Files used in the last few weeks

Explore your hard drive

Shortcuts on the desktop

Files and Web pages in your Favorites folder

Files on your organisation's Web server

Finding files

When there are lots of files in a **Look in** area, it can be hard to spot the one you want. Here are three ways simplify the job.

● Setting the **Files of type** box to the correct type will filter out swathes of unwanted stuff.

● If you know part of the name, type it in the **File name** box and press [Enter]. Only files that contains those characters will be displayed:

e.g. '*memo*' would list '*memo* to boss.doc', '29june *memo*.txt', '*memo*ry costs.xls'

If you are unsure about some characters, fill the gap with an asterisk (*) – this is a 'wildcard', that can stand for any characters:

e.g. '*chap*2*' would find '*chap*ter2.doc', '*chap*ter20.doc', '*chap*el choir May 12.txt'

● In the Details display, you can list files by Name, Size, Type or Date – just click on the header to list in ascending order, and click again for descending order.

The Find panel

If you have forgotten a file's name, or where you stored it, the Find panel is the answer. This will look through the properties and contents of files to find matching words. It can also search through subfolders – so if it's somewhere on the disk, it will be found!

Basic steps

1 Select the Look in area and folder, if known.

2 If you know part or all of the Name, enter it.

3 Specify the File type if known, otherwise set this to All files.

4 Click the ⊞▾ button and select Details.

5 Click a header to sort the list into order.

❑ If it isn't found...

6 Open the Tools menu and select Find.

7 Select a Property, e.g. *Contents* and set the Condition and Value to be matched, then click [Add to List].

8 Set the Look in: to a higher level folder, or the top of the drive.

9 Click [Find Now].

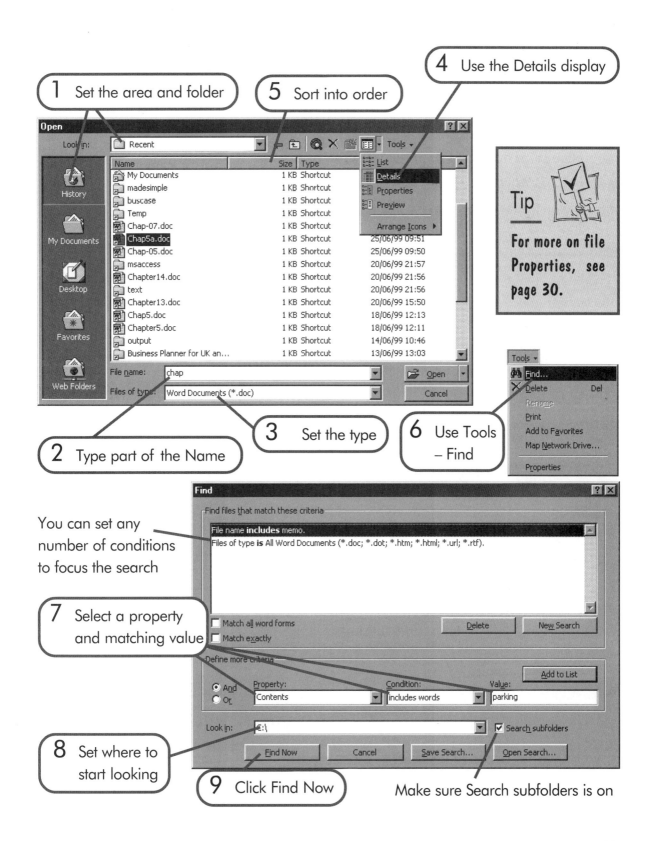

1 Set the area and folder

5 Sort into order

4 Use the Details display

Open

Look in: Recent

Name	Size	Type
My Documents	1 KB	Shortcut
madesimple	1 KB	Shortcut
buscase	1 KB	Shortcut
Temp	1 KB	Shortcut
Chap-07.doc	1 KB	Shortcut
Chap5a.doc	1 KB	Shortcut
Chap-05.doc	1 KB	Shortcut
msaccess	1 KB	Shortcut
Chapter14.doc	1 KB	Shortcut
text	1 KB	Shortcut
Chapter13.doc	1 KB	Shortcut
Chap5.doc	1 KB	Shortcut
Chapter5.doc	1 KB	Shortcut
output	1 KB	Shortcut
Business Planner for UK an...	1 KB	Shortcut

Tools ▾
List
Details
Properties
Preview
Arrange Icons ▶

25/06/99 09:51
25/06/99 09:50
20/06/99 21:57
20/06/99 21:56
20/06/99 21:56
20/06/99 15:50
18/06/99 12:13
18/06/99 12:11
14/06/99 10:46
13/06/99 13:03

History
My Documents
Desktop
Favorites
Web Folders

File name: chap   Open
Files of type: Word Documents (*.doc)   Cancel

Tip

For more on file Properties, see page 30.

Tools ▾
Find...
Delete   Del
Rename
Print
Add to Favorites
Map Network Drive...
Properties

3 Set the type

6 Use Tools – Find

2 Type part of the Name

Find

You can set any number of conditions to focus the search

Find files that match these criteria

File name **includes** memo.
Files of type **is** All Word Documents (*.doc; *.dot; *.htm; *.html; *.url; *.rtf).

☐ Match all word forms   Delete   New Search
☐ Match exactly

7 Select a property and matching value

Define more criteria

Add to List

⦿ And   Property: Condition: Value:
○ Or   Contents   includes words   parking

Look in: C:\   ☑ Search subfolders

8 Set where to start looking

Find Now   Cancel   Save Search...   Open Search...

9 Click Find Now

Make sure Search subfolders is on

27

Saving files

There are two file-saving routines in Office applications.

- **Save** is used to save an existing file after editing – just click 🖫 or open the **File** menu and select **Save**.

- **Save As** is used to save a new file, or to save an existing file with a new name or in a new folder – see the steps.

2 Use File – Save As

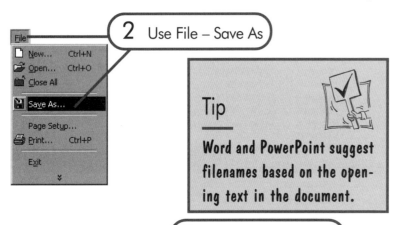

Tip

Word and PowerPoint suggest filenames based on the opening text in the document.

Basic steps

1 Click 🖫 to save a new file.

Or

2 Open the File menu and select Save As to save a file with a new name or location.

3 Set the Save in folder.

4 Enter the Filename.

5 Change the Save as type setting if required.

6 Click 🖫 Save .

7 Return to editing, or exit, as desired.

3 Switch to the folder

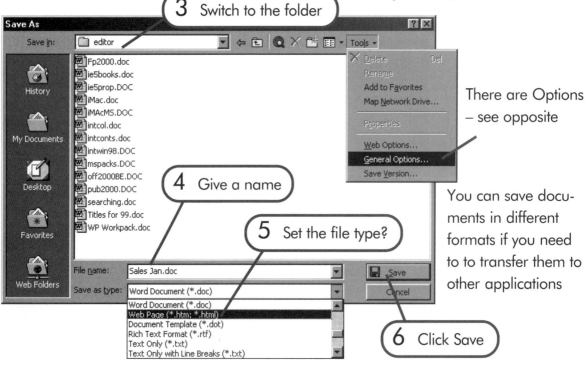

4 Give a name

5 Set the file type?

6 Click Save

There are Options – see opposite

You can save documents in different formats if you need to to transfer them to other applications

Save options

Tools – General Options on the **Save** panel opens an extensive Options panel in Word and a simpler one in Excel. PowerPoint allows no options for individual files, though you can set defaults on the **Save** tab of the **Tools – Options** panel. The key options are those which protect the file:

Password to open, prevents all unauthorised access;

Password to modify allows anyone to read it, but only the password holder can save it, with the same name;

Read recommended sets Ready Only as the default mode for opening the file.

If you have any doubts about the PC's reliability, turn on the Always create Backup option

PowerPoint also lets you Embed True Type fonts, to ensure that the document looks the same on any PC

Background saves and Save AutoRecover guard against lost work – set a reasonable interval

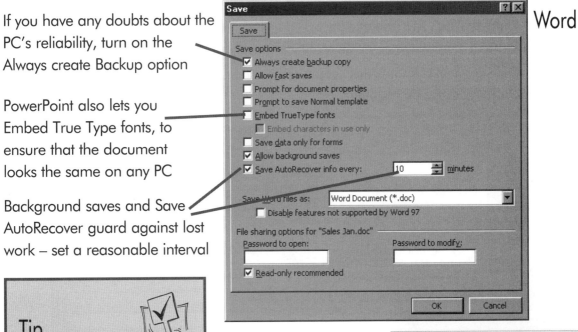

Word

Excel

File properties

All Office 2000 files have Properties panels which contain information about the nature of the file. These can be viewed when opening files (see page 24) and searched in the Find routine (see page 26).

- The **General** tab holds the basic details of the file – location, size, date saved, etc.;

- The basic information on the **Summary** panel is produced by Office 2000 – fill in the blanks as required and tick **Save preview picture** if wanted;

- On the **Statistics** panel, the Words count is useful for students, journalists or anyone else working to a set limit;

- The **Contents** lists the headings in a Word document, slide titles in a presentation, or sheets in an Excel book;

- The **Custom** panel can hold other details of the document – this is for advanced users only!

Basic steps

1 Open the File menu and select Properties.

2 Switch to the Summary panel.

3 Enter information as required – the Subject and Keywords will be useful in future Finds.

4 Turn on Save Preview Picture if this will help to identify the file later.

5 Click [OK].

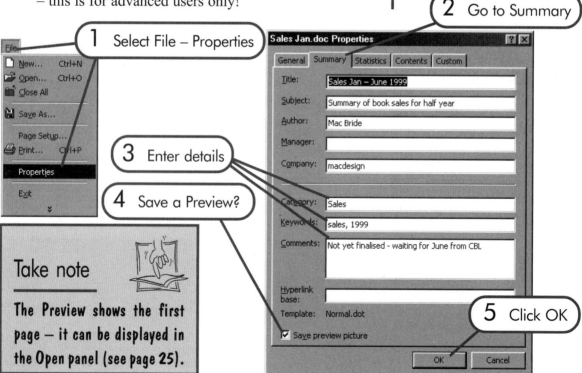

1 Select File – Properties

2 Go to Summary

3 Enter details

4 Save a Preview?

5 Click OK

Take note

The Preview shows the first page – it can be displayed in the Open panel (see page 25).

Take note

You must save the file (again) after filling in the Properties, to save the information.

The Contents are generated only if Save Preview picture is checked.

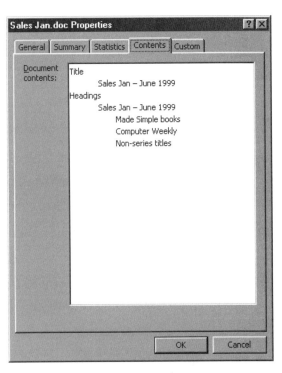

On the Statistics panel, don't believe the Total editing time figure, it is simply how long the file was open!

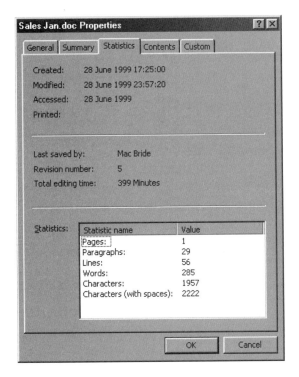

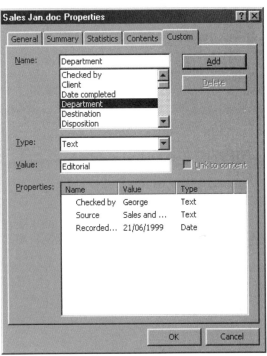

To add Custom information, select the Name and Type, enter the Value and click Add.

Summary

- ❏ All commands can be accessed through the menus, and all the common ones through the toolbars.

- ❏ Many of the items on the menus and toolbars are the same in all Office applications.

- ❏ Commands can be added to or removed from menus.

- ❏ The Standard and Formatting toolbars are normally displayed. Other ones can be brought onto the screen as and when they are needed.

- ❏ Files can be opened from the Shortcut bar or from within applications.

- ❏ The File finding facility helps you to track down files if you have forgotten their names or folders.

- ❏ There are templates and wizards available to simplify setting up new documents.

- ❏ When saving files for the first time, you must specify a folder and filename through the Save As dialog box. Resaving simply takes a click on the Save button.

- ❏ When saving a file, if you save its Preview, you will make it easier to find it when you want to open it in the future.

- ❏ A file's Properties panel can hold summary data and a description of the file.

3 Help!

Office Assistant

Office Assistant is a friendly front-end to the Help system. It keeps an eye on what you are doing, so that, when you call on it for help, it will be ready with some likely topics. If it has guessed wrong – as it often does – you simply tell it what you need help with, and it will come up with the goods.

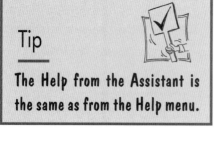

Tip

The Help from the Assistant is the same as from the Help menu.

Basic steps

1   If the Assistant is not visible, click the query icon to wake it up.

2   If a relevant topic is listed, click on it to display the page.

Otherwise

3   Type a word or phrase to describe the Help you want.

4   Click Search.

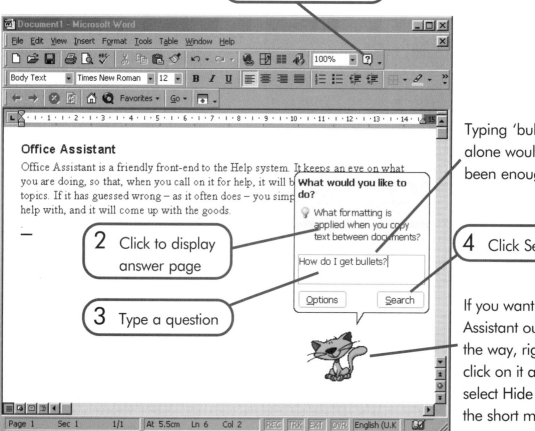

1   Wake the Assistant

Office Assistant

Office Assistant is a friendly front-end to the Help system. It keeps an eye on what you are doing, so that, when you call on it for help, it will be topics. If it has guessed wrong – as it often does – you simp help with, and it will come up with the goods.

What would you like to do?

What formatting is applied when you copy text between documents?

How do I get bullets?

Options   Search

2   Click to display answer page

3   Type a question

Typing 'bullets' alone would have been enough

4   Click Search

If you want the Assistant out of the way, right-click on it and select Hide from the short menu

34

5 You will be offered a list of topics – click the one that is closest to your question.

6 If you are offered a set of links to pages, click on one to read it.

7 Read the page, following any underlined links if they look useful.

8 Click 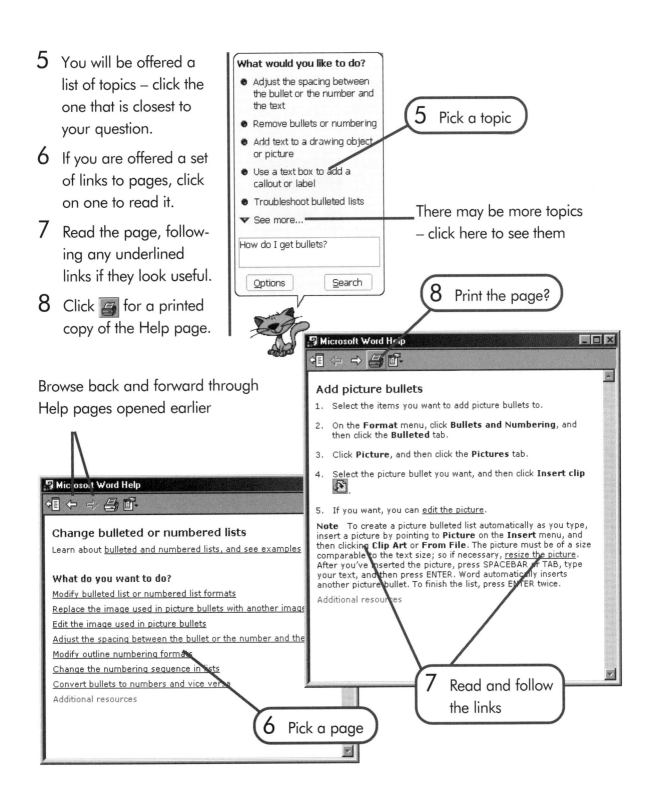 for a printed copy of the Help page.

Browse back and forward through Help pages opened earlier

What would you like to do?

● Adjust the spacing between the bullet or the number and the text

● Remove bullets or numbering

● Add text to a drawing object or picture

● Use a text box to add a callout or label

● Troubleshoot bulleted lists

▼ See more...

How do I get bullets?

[Options]   [Search]

5 Pick a topic

There may be more topics – click here to see them

8 Print the page?

Microsoft Word Help

Add picture bullets

1. Select the items you want to add picture bullets to.

2. On the **Format** menu, click **Bullets and Numbering**, and then click the **Bulleted** tab.

3. Click **Picture**, and then click the **Pictures** tab.

4. Select the picture bullet you want, and then click **Insert clip** [icon].

5. If you want, you can edit the picture.

Note To create a picture bulleted list automatically as you type, insert a picture by pointing to **Picture** on the **Insert** menu, and then clicking **Clip Art** or **From File**. The picture must be of a size comparable to the text size; so if necessary, resize the picture. After you've inserted the picture, press SPACEBAR or TAB, type your text, and then press ENTER. Word automatically inserts another picture bullet. To finish the list, press ENTER twice.

Additional resources

Microsoft Word Help

Change bulleted or numbered lists

Learn about bulleted and numbered lists, and see examples

What do you want to do?

Modify bulleted list or numbered list formats
Replace the image used in picture bullets with another image
Edit the image used in picture bullets
Adjust the spacing between the bullet or the number and the
Modify outline numbering formats
Change the numbering sequence in lists
Convert bullets to numbers and vice versa
Additional resources

7 Read and follow the links

6 Pick a page

35

Customising Office Assistant

The Assistant has eight alternative 'personalities' for you to choose from, and – rather more usefully – a set of options to control how it works. And you can turn it off completely if you find it more irritating than entertaining!

The Logo is the least obtrusive

The Genius is one of the best animations

Basic steps

1 Click Options on the Assistant's dialog or on its right-click menu.

2 Select an image on the Gallery panel.

3 Set the Options as required.

4 Click [OK].

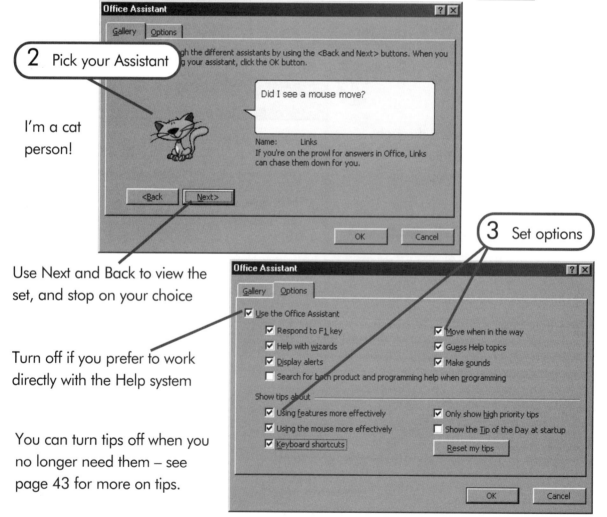

2 Pick your Assistant

I'm a cat person!

Use Next and Back to view the set, and stop on your choice

Turn off if you prefer to work directly with the Help system

You can turn tips off when you no longer need them – see page 43 for more on tips.

3 Set options

The Help menu

The Help system is the same in all applications, only the first item varies

These two are normally hidden – you may never need either of them

This is the route into the full Help system. The menu has seven options, of which five are immediately visible:

- ***application* Help** opens the Help system or displays the Office Assistant if used – the [?] button also opens this;
- **Show/Hide Office Assistant** toggles its display,
- **What's This?** provides quick explanations of the buttons and options on the main screen and on dialog boxes;
- **Office on the Web** links to pages at Microsoft's Web site. These are mainly for new Web users, but if you cannot find the answers you need in the built-in Help – and if you have an Internet connection – you might try here;
- **About *application*** displays copyright and other details – there's also a link to Technical Support;

If you click [»], two more options appear.

- **WordPerfect Help** provides special assistance for users converting from WordPerfect, showing the WordPerfect command keystrokes and their equivalent Word commands and keyboard shortcuts.
- **Detect and Repair** check the application and restores any lost or corrupted program files – you will need your Office CD if you want to use this.

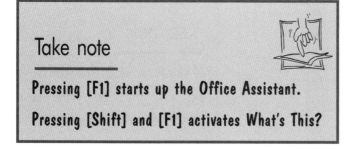

Take note

Pressing [F1] starts up the Office Assistant.

Pressing [Shift] and [F1] activates What's This?

The Help system

If you use the Office Assistant to access the Help system, all you normally see is a page of Help, but there is more to it than this. Click 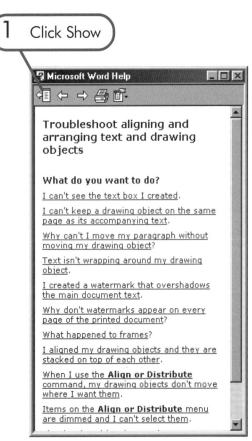 the Show button, on the left of the toolbar, and a new panel opens. Its tabs gives you three ways to find Help.

Contents tab

This approach treats the Help pages as a book. Scan through the headings to find a section that seems to cover what you want, and open that to see the page titles. (Some sections have sub-sections, making it a 2 or 3-stage process to get to page titles.)

Some Help topics are stand-alone pages; some have a top page with a set of links to pages on different aspects of the topic.

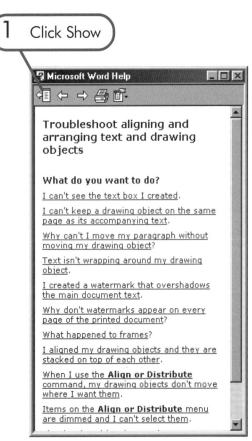

1 Click Show

Microsoft Word Help

Troubleshoot aligning and arranging text and drawing objects

What do you want to do?

I can't see the text box I created.

I can't keep a drawing object on the same page as its accompanying text.

Why can't I move my paragraph without moving my drawing object?

Text isn't wrapping around my drawing object.

I created a watermark that overshadows the main document text.

Why don't watermarks appear on every page of the printed document?

What happened to frames?

I aligned my drawing objects and they are stacked on top of each other.

When I use the **Align or Distribute** command, my drawing objects don't move where I want them.

Items on the **Align or Distribute** menu are dimmed and I can't select them.

Basic steps

1 Click ⬛ the Show button.

2 Click the Contents tab if this panel is not at the front already.

3 Click ⊞ open a book – or ⊟ to close one.

4 Click ? or the page title to see a page.

5 Click on <u>underlined text</u> to go to the linked page – following up links as necessary.

6 Use the ⬅ and ➡ buttons to move be-tween visited pages.

7 When you have found the Help you want, click on the application window to hide Help or click ✕ to close Help.

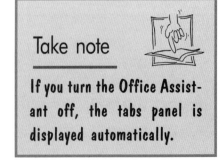

Take note

If you turn the Office Assist-ant off, the tabs panel is displayed automatically.

Click to hide the tabs if you
want them out of the way

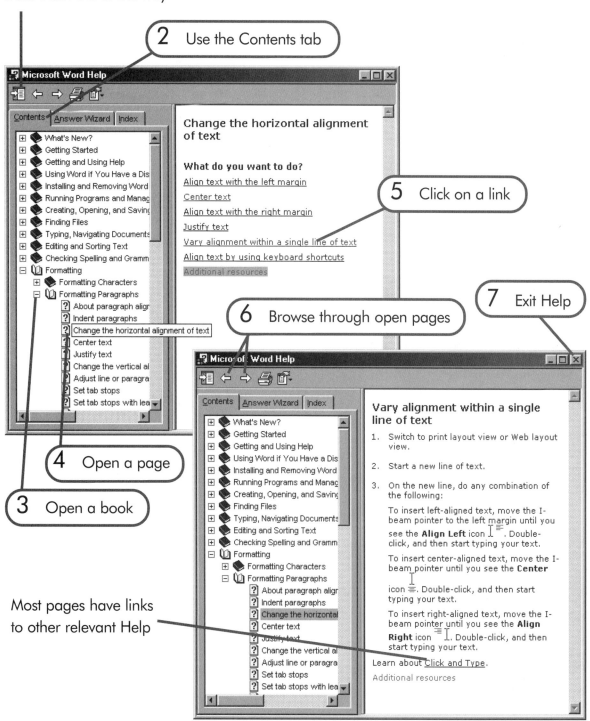

2   Use the Contents tab

Microsoft Word Help

Contents   Answer Wizard   Index

- ⊞ 📕 What's New?
- ⊞ 📕 Getting Started
- ⊞ 📕 Getting and Using Help
- ⊞ 📕 Using Word if You Have a Dis
- ⊞ 📕 Installing and Removing Word
- ⊞ 📕 Running Programs and Manag
- ⊞ 📕 Creating, Opening, and Saving
- ⊞ 📕 Finding Files
- ⊞ 📕 Typing, Navigating Documents
- ⊞ 📕 Editing and Sorting Text
- ⊞ 📕 Checking Spelling and Gramm
- ⊟ 📖 Formatting
  - ⊞ 📕 Formatting Characters
  - ⊟ 📖 Formatting Paragraphs
    - ❓ About paragraph align
    - ❓ Indent paragraphs
    - ❓ Change the horizontal alignment of text
    - ❓ Center text
    - ❓ Justify text
    - ❓ Change the vertical al
    - ❓ Adjust line or paragra
    - ❓ Set tab stops
    - ❓ Set tab stops with lea

Change the horizontal alignment of text

What do you want to do?

Align text with the left margin

Center text

Align text with the right margin

Justify text

Vary alignment within a single line of text

Align text by using keyboard shortcuts

Additional resources

5   Click on a link

7   Exit Help

6   Browse through open pages

4   Open a page

3   Open a book

Microsoft Word Help

Contents   Answer Wizard   Index

- ⊞ 📕 What's New?
- ⊞ 📕 Getting Started
- ⊞ 📕 Getting and Using Help
- ⊞ 📕 Using Word if You Have a Dis
- ⊞ 📕 Installing and Removing Word
- ⊞ 📕 Running Programs and Manag
- ⊞ 📕 Creating, Opening, and Saving
- ⊞ 📕 Finding Files
- ⊞ 📕 Typing, Navigating Documents
- ⊞ 📕 Editing and Sorting Text
- ⊞ 📕 Checking Spelling and Gramm
- ⊟ 📖 Formatting
  - ⊞ 📕 Formatting Characters
  - ⊟ 📖 Formatting Paragraphs
    - ❓ About paragraph align
    - ❓ Indent paragraphs
    - ❓ Change the horizontal
    - ❓ Center text
    - ❓ Justify text
    - ❓ Change the vertical al
    - ❓ Adjust line or paragra
    - ❓ Set tab stops
    - ❓ Set tab stops with lea

Vary alignment within a single line of text

1. Switch to print layout view or Web layout view.

2. Start a new line of text.

3. On the new line, do any combination of the following:

   To insert left-aligned text, move the I-beam pointer to the left margin until you see the **Align Left** icon. Double-click, and then start typing your text.

   To insert center-aligned text, move the I-beam pointer until you see the **Center** icon. Double-click, and then start typing your text.

   To insert right-aligned text, move the I-beam pointer until you see the **Align Right** icon. Double-click, and then start typing your text.

Learn about Click and Type.

Additional resources

Most pages have links
to other relevant Help

Answer Wizard

This is almost identical to asking a question through the Office Assistant. The main difference is that all the possible topics are displayed in the panel.

You can type in complete questions, or simply the most significant words. In the example below 'table columns change' produces exactly the same set of topics as 'How do I change columns in a table?'

Basic steps

1 Switch to the Answer Wizard tab.

2 Type a word or phrase to describe the Help you want.

3 Click Search.

4 You will be offered a list of topics – click the one that is closest to your question.

5 If you are offered a set of links to pages, click on one to read it.

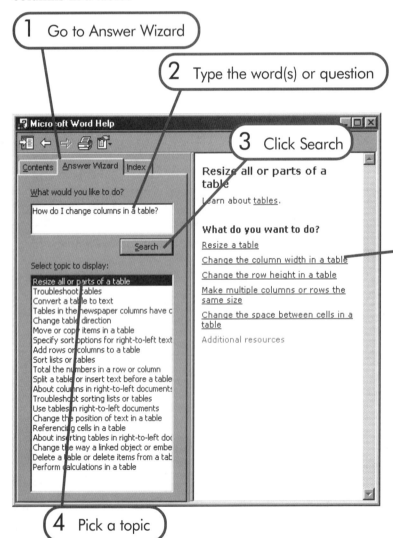

> 1 Go to Answer Wizard
>
> 2 Type the word(s) or question
>
> 3 Click Search
>
> 5 Follow the links
>
> 4 Pick a topic

Take note

If there is only one relevant topic page, the system will take you directly to it after Step 4.

Using the Index

1 Click the Index tab.

2 Start to type a word in the keyword box, then select it from the list.

3 Click [Search].

4 Enter a second word and search again.

5 Select a topic.

The Answer Wizard will locate the main Help pages on any topic, but if you want to dig deeper, try the Index. Searching for a word here will track down every page on which it occurs – and the Help system is very thoroughly indexcd! The best way to use it is to give two or more words, to focus onto the most relevant pages.

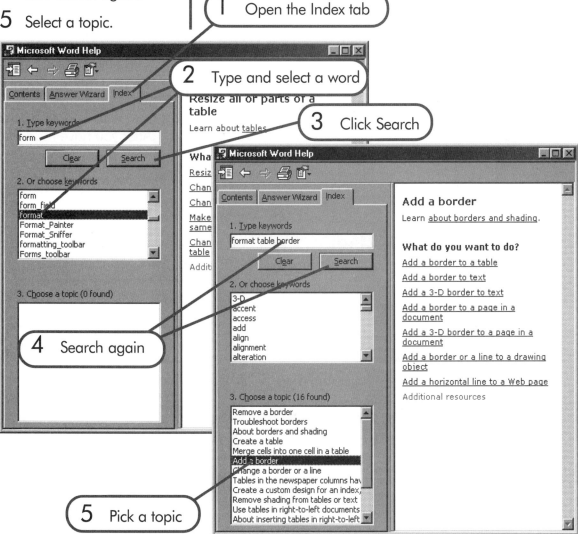

1 Open the Index tab

2 Type and select a word

3 Click Search

4 Search again

5 Pick a topic

What's This?

Office's icons, menus and dialog boxes are designed to be intuitive – which is great, as long as you know how to intuit! However, when you first start to use these applications, you may need a little prompting. *What's This?* will tell you about the buttons and menu items in the main application window.

Once you open a dialog box or menu, you can no longer get to the What's This? command, but the Help is still at hand. Most dialog boxes have a query icon [?] at the top right, which does the same job, and – no matter what you are doing – pressing **[Shift]** and **[F1]** will usually start the What's This? Help.

Basic steps

❑ In the main window

1 Open the Help menu and select What's This?

❑ On a dialog box

2 Click ▣ or ▾?.

❑ On a menu (or any-where)

3 Press [Shift] – [F1].

4 Click the ▾? cursor on the item that you want to know about.

5 After you have read the Help box, click any-where to close it.

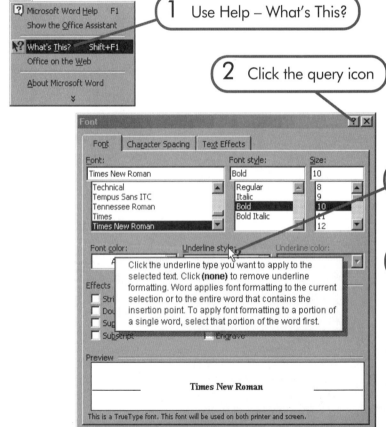

1 Use Help – What's This?

2 Click the query icon

4 Point and click for Help

5 Click anywhere to close

Click the underline type you want to apply to the selected text. Click **(none)** to remove underline formatting. Word applies font formatting to the current selection or to the entire word that contains the insertion point. To apply font formatting to a portion of a single word, select that portion of the word first.

Take note

You only get one Help box each time you use What's This?

42

Tips and ScreenTips

❑ When the light is on

1 Click on the Office Assistant or the light icon to get the tip.

2 Select the new – or an earlier – tip.

3 If the tips don't help, ask a question and search as normal.

Tip

The startup Tip of the Day, and 'low priority' tips can be turned off through the Assistant's Options – see page 36.

If ever you see 💡 on Office Assistant, it has a tip related to your last action or to the last error report. The tips that crop up during a session are stored in the bubble, and can be read at any time

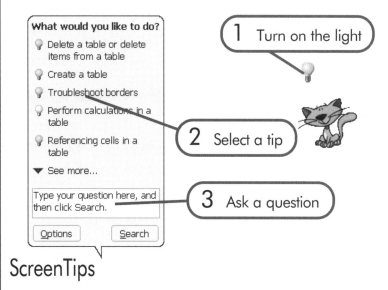

1 Turn on the light

2 Select a tip

3 Ask a question

ScreenTips

These are little prompts that appear when you pause the mouse over a tool button, to tell you its name and its shortcut keys. The tips can be turned on or off through the **Options** tab of the **Toolbars – Customize** dialog box.

Use Tools – Customize to open this dialog box

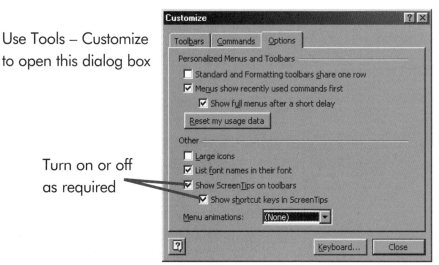

Turn on or off as required

If you mainly work through the keyboard, not the mouse, the shortcuts save time

Summary

❑ Help is always available.

❑ Office Assistant is a friendly front-end to the Help system. It will offer appropriate Help when needed, and can handle questions written in simple English.

❑ Office Assistant has several 'personalities' – choose the one that suits you.

❑ Use the Contents panel when you are browsing to see what topics are covered.

❑ You can get Help by asking a question in the Answer Wizard tab – it works the same as asking the Assistant.

❑ Use the Index to go directly to the Help on a specified operation or object.

❑ For help in a dialog box or panel, use What's this? or click the query icon and point to the item.

❑ If you hold the cursor over an icon, a brief prompt will pop up to tell you what it does.

❑ The Tip of the Day at start up can be switched off if no longer wanted. Tips are stored and can be reviewed at any time.

4 Word

Introducing Word 2000

Word is the world's leading word-processor, and with Word 2000, its dominance is set to continue. It can be used to produce just about any text-based document – letters, flyers, Web pages, reports, newsletters, even books (complete with contents, index and footnotes)! For the most part it is remarkably easy to use – and the trickier operations are those which most people will rarely need. To make things even easier, Word is equipped with dozens of templates and wizards which provide the style, layout and suggested contents for a wide range of documents.

The Word window

The bulk of the space is taken up, of course, by the working area where you type your text, and insert graphics and other objects to create your documents. Around this area are:

- The **Title bar**, showing the name of the document, and carrying the usual Minimize, Maximize/Restore and Close application buttons.

- The **Menu bar**, giving you access to all of Word's many features. At the far right is the Close button – click to close the document, but keep Word active (this is not present when a document is opened in a new window).

- The **toolbars** – normally just the Standard and Formatting toolbars, but others can be displayed as required. The toolbars are usually on the top and side of the working area, but can be moved or floated (see page 18).

- The **scroll bars**, used for moving around your document – just drag the sliders or click the arrows at the ends to scroll the display. At the bottom of the right scroll bar are buttons for switching between pages; and at the the left of the bottom bar are four buttons for changing the view.

Take note

If you know what you want to say, Word will help you to say it better, and give a professional gloss to your documents.

Take note

This chapter only covers those aspects of Word that are unique to Word. For more on working with text and other objects, see Chapters 7 to 9.

are not present in some views (see page 48).

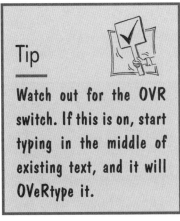

Tip

Watch out for the OVR switch. If this is on, start typing in the middle of existing text, and it will OVeRtype it.

● The **rulers**, showing the margins, indents and tabs. These are not present in some views (see page 48).

● The **Status bar** helps to keep you informed. It shows where you are in the document, what language the spell checker (see page 122) is using, and the state of various switches.

Title bar   Menu bar   Toolbars   Ruler   Minimize   Maximize/Restore   Close Word

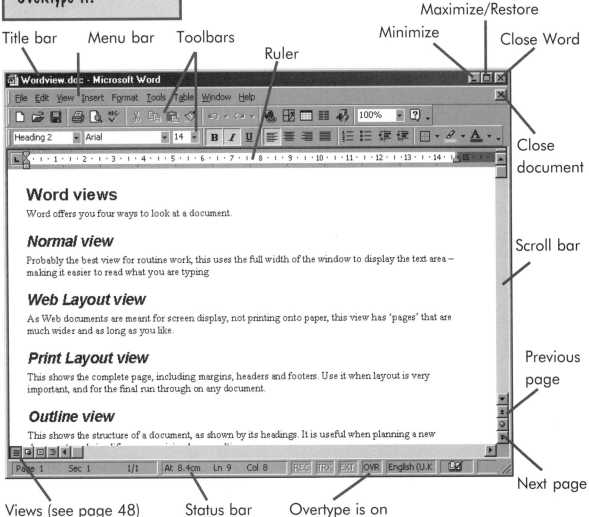

Close document

Scroll bar

Previous page

Next page

Views (see page 48)   Status bar   Overtype is on

Word views

Word offers you four ways to look at a document.

Normal view
Probably the best view for routine work, this uses the full width of the window to display the text area – making it easier to read what you are typing. The screenshot on page 47 shows Word in Normal view.

Web Layout view
As Web documents are meant for screen display, not printing onto paper, this view has 'pages' that are much wider and as long as you like.

Print Layout view
This shows the complete page, including margins, headers and footers. Use it when layout is very important, and for the final run-through on any document.

Outline view
This shows the structure of a document, as shown by its headings. It is useful when planning a new document, and simplifies reorganising long, multi-page ones.

Changing views

To switch between views, use the buttons at the bottom left of the screen, or the options on the View menu.

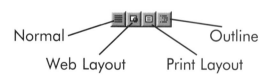

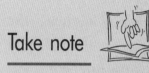

Take note

You can do most jobs — edit and format text, insert pictures, run a spell check, and many more — in all four views.

This means that you can put the finishing touches to a document while looking at it in Web or Print Layout view.

Web Layout view

Print Layout view

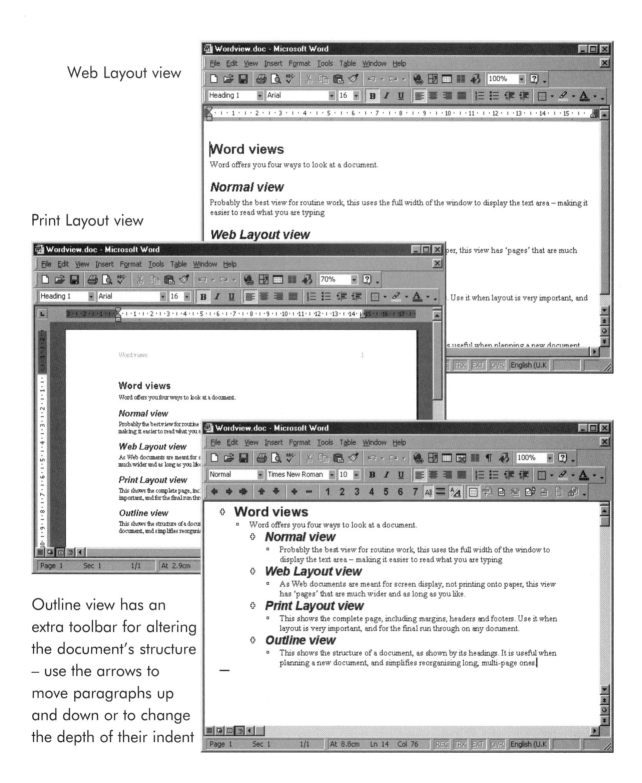

Outline view has an extra toolbar for altering the document's structure – use the arrows to move paragraphs up and down or to change the depth of their indent

Documents and templates

All documents start from some kind of template which sets up the basic design. Even the 'blank document' is a template, though this simply sets the page size and the fonts for the normal and heading text. Other templates have more elaborate design features and suggestions for content and layout of the items to include in the new document.

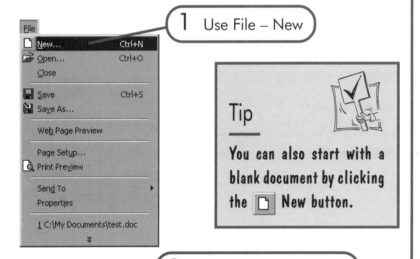

1   Use File – New

Tip

You can also start with a blank document by clicking the ☐ New button.

2   Select Blank Document

1   Open the File menu and select New.

❏   Blank document

2   At the New dialog box, select *Blank Document* on the General tab.

3   Click   OK .

❏   Using a template

4   Select a tab.

5   Click on a template to see its preview.

6   When you find a suitable template, click   OK .

7   Click into the prompts and replace them with your own details.

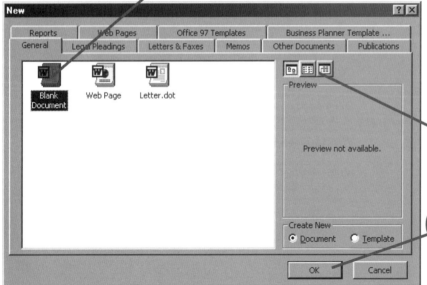

Click to view the templates in a simple list or with the file details

3   Click OK

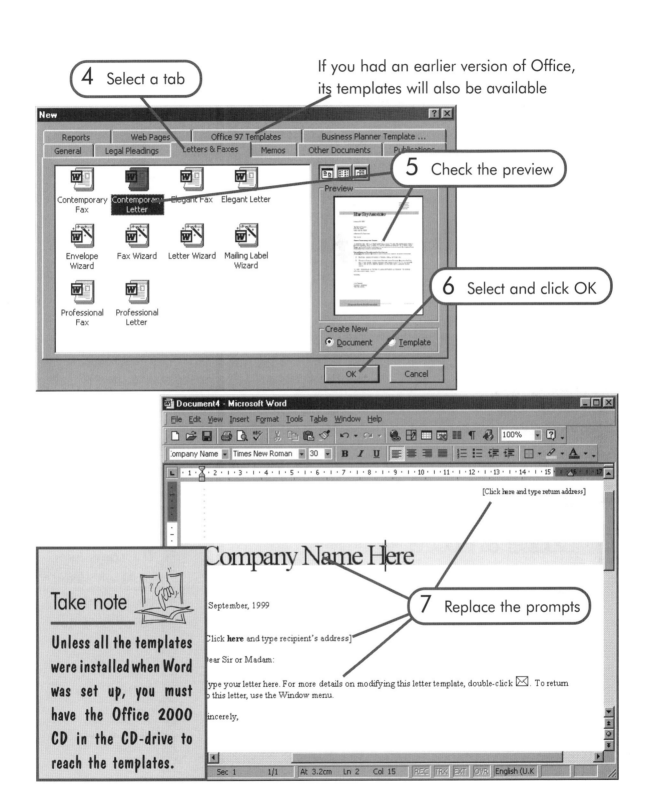

4 Select a tab

If you had an earlier version of Office, its templates will also be available

New

Reports | Web Pages | Office 97 Templates | Business Planner Template ...
General | Legal Pleadings | Letters & Faxes | Memos | Other Documents | Publications

Contemporary Fax | Contemporary Letter | Elegant Fax | Elegant Letter

Envelope Wizard | Fax Wizard | Letter Wizard | Mailing Label Wizard

Professional Fax | Professional Letter

Preview

5 Check the preview

Create New
● Document   ○ Template

6 Select and click OK

OK | Cancel

Document4 - Microsoft Word

File Edit View Insert Format Tools Table Window Help

Company Name | Times New Roman | 30 | **B** *I* U

[Click here and type return address]

Company Name Here

September, 1999

7 Replace the prompts

[Click **here** and type recipient's address]

Dear Sir or Madam:

Type your letter here. For more details on modifying this letter template, double-click ✉. To return to this letter, use the Window menu.

Sincerely,

Sec 1 | 1/1 | At 3.2cm | Ln 2 | Col 15 | REC TRK EXT OVR | English (U.K

Take note

Unless all the templates were installed when Word was set up, you must have the Office 2000 CD in the CD-drive to reach the templates.

Sample letter
based on the
Contemporary
Letter template

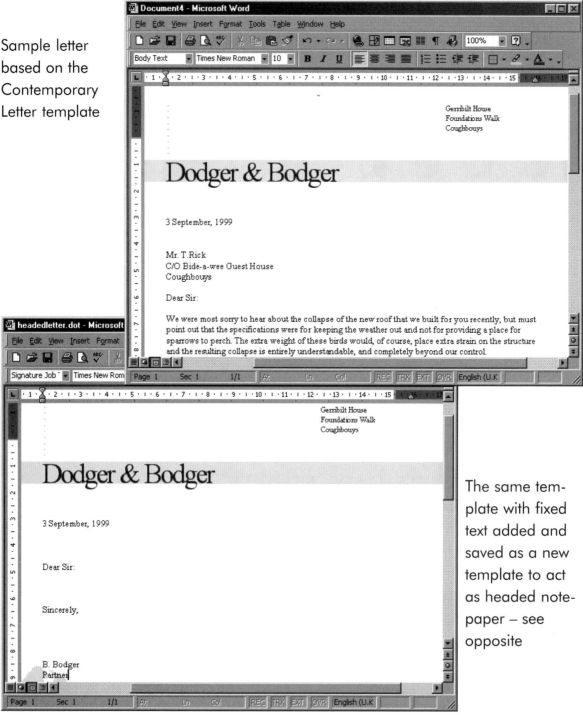

The same tem-
plate with fixed
text added and
saved as a new
template to act
as headed note-
paper – see
opposite

Making your own templates

1 Starting from a template or blank document, enter the fixed text and other items.

2 Open the File menu and select Save As…

3 From the Save as type drop-down list select *Document template*.

4 Enter a filename.

5 Click 🖫 Save .

❑ Your template can be opened from the New dialog box.

This is so easy, and so useful, that you should explore it early on in your use of Word. You can create your own templates for everything from headed notepaper to draft contracts. All you need to do is set up a document with a suitable design and layout and all the fixed information, but leave out any specific details – the name of the person, the quote for the job, the text of the letter, and so forth – then save it the right way.

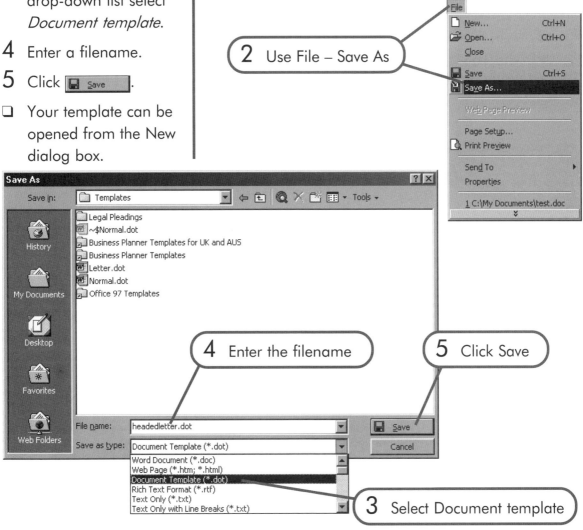

2 Use File – Save As

4 Enter the filename

5 Click Save

3 Select Document template

Document wizards

In amongst the ordinary templates are a number of wizards which offer alternative ways to start new documents. They tend to be used where there are more optional elements – setting them through a wizard means that the basic document is closer to what you want than a normal template could be.

Wizards are simple to use, and all work along the same lines.

● Where there are alternatives, click the button by the one you want:

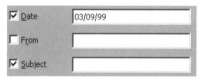

● Where an item is optional, tick the box to include it in the layout. The data to be displayed should be entered if you are creating a document, but left blank if this is a template and the data is not a fixed item.

☑ Date	03/09/99
☐ From	
☑ Subject	

Here, for example, is the Memo wizard in action.

1 At the New dialog box, select the wizard you require.

2 Work through the wizard, setting the options or entering details at the prompts.

3 Click `Next >` to move on to the next stage.

4 Click `< Back` if you need to go back to the previous stage.

5 Click `Finish` when done.

You can also work through the wizard by clicking the blocks to go direct to a stage – handy if you've used the wizard before and know that you want to skip some stages.

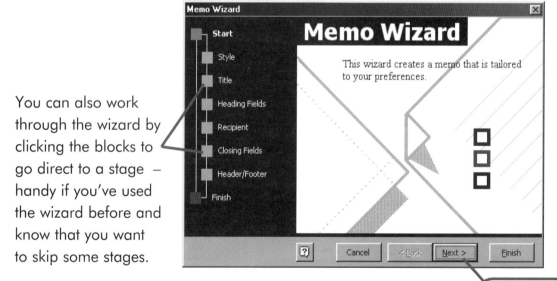

3 Click Next

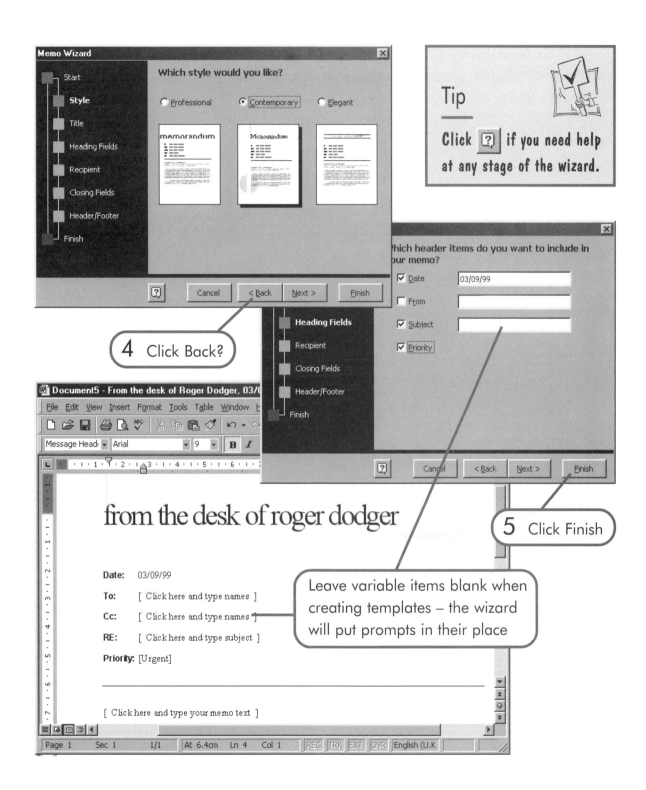

Memo Wizard

- Start
- **Style**
- Title
- Heading Fields
- Recipient
- Closing Fields
- Header/Footer
- Finish

Which style would you like?

○ Professional   ⦿ Contemporary   ○ Elegant

memorandum   Memorandum

Cancel   < Back   Next >   Finish

Tip

Click ⏹ if you need help at any stage of the wizard.

Which header items do you want to include in your memo?

☑ Date   03/09/99
☐ From
☑ Subject
☑ Priority

- **Heading Fields**
- Recipient
- Closing Fields
- Header/Footer
- Finish

Cancel   < Back   Next >   Finish

4 Click Back?

5 Click Finish

Document5 - From the desk of Roger Dodger, 03/0

File Edit View Insert Format Tools Table Window H

Message Head ▾ Arial ▾ 9 ▾ **B** *I*

from the desk of roger dodger

Date: 03/09/99

To: [Click here and type names]

Cc: [Click here and type names]

RE: [Click here and type subject]

Priority: [Urgent]

_____

[Click here and type your memo text]

Leave variable items blank when creating templates – the wizard will put prompts in their place

Page 1   Sec 1   1/1   At 6.4cm   Ln 4   Col 1   REC TRK EXT OVR   English (U.K

Columns

Word's layout facilities are almost as good as you will find in dedicated DTP (desktop publishing) software – its handling of columns is a good example.

You can set text in two or three columns, of the same or different widths, over the whole document or a selected part.

1 Select the text to set in columns, or the point where you want the columns to start.

2 Open the Format menu and select Columns…

3 Select the closest Preset design.

4 Clear Equal spacing and adjust the Width or Spacing if wanted.

5 Tick Line between if required.

6 Set the Apply to option.

7 Click OK.

1 Select the text or the start point?

2 Use Format – Columns

3 Pick a Preset

7 Click OK

4 Adjust widths and spacing?

5 Line between?

6 Apply to what?

Documents can be split into sections for easier handling

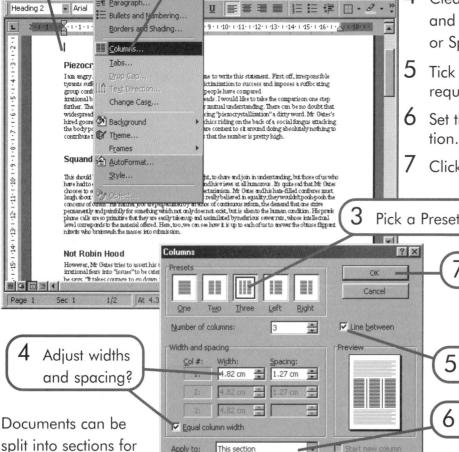

56

Headers and footers

Basic steps

1 Open the View menu and select Header and Footer.

2 Click into the header.

3 Open the Insert menu and select Page Numbers, Date and Time or an Autotext entry.

4 Add any other text then format as usual.

5 Repeat for the footer.

6 Click into the main text to return to normal editing.

Headers and footers are a useful addition to documents of more than one page. At the very least, you can use them to display the page numbers, but the title, date, filename and other information can also be displayed here.

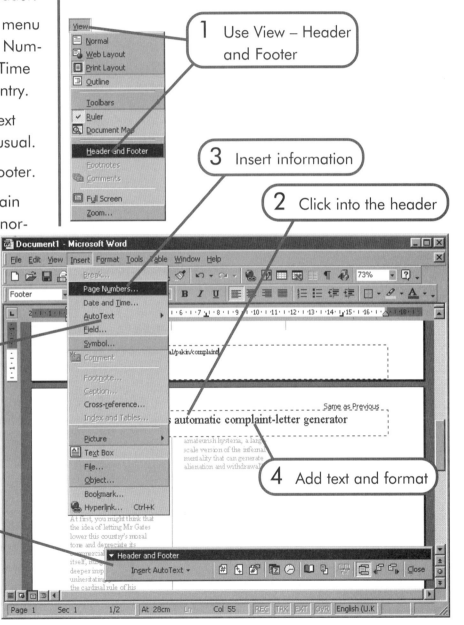

> 1 Use View – Header and Footer

> 3 Insert information

> 2 Click into the header

> 4 Add text and format

Document details can be selected from the Autotext submenu

Items can also be inserted from the Header and Footer toolbar

Styles

A *style* is a combination of font, size, alignment and indent options. Word has a range of pre-defined styles, and you can modify these or add your own. Applying a style is a matter of a couple of clicks; creating a new style is almost as simple.

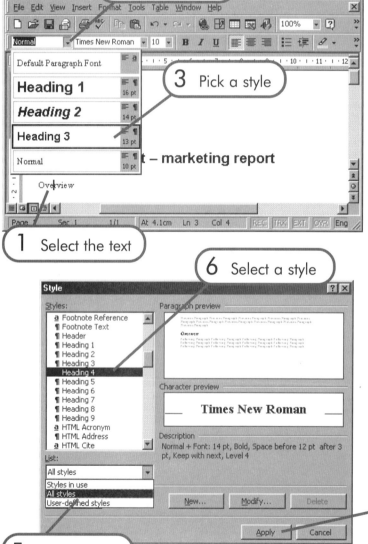

Basic steps

❏ Applying a style

1 Select the paragraph – styles apply to whole paragraphs.

2 Open the Styles list.

3 Pick one from the list

or

4 Open the Format menu and select Style…

5 List All styles.

6 Pick from the long list.

7 Click ▭Apply▭.

2 Open the list

3 Pick a style

t – marketing report

Overview

1 Select the text

6 Select a style

4 Use Format – Style

5 List All styles

7 Click Apply

❑ Modifying a style

1 At the Style dialog box, pick the style.

2 Click [Modify...].

3 Click [Format ▾].

4 Select an aspect and edit the settings.

5 Repeat 3 and 4 as necessary.

6 Click [OK].

7 Click [Apply] at the Style dialog box.

❑ Creating a style

8 At the Style dialog box, click [New...].

9 Type in a Name then follow steps 3 to 7.

Take note

For more on formatting, see Chapter 7, Working with text.

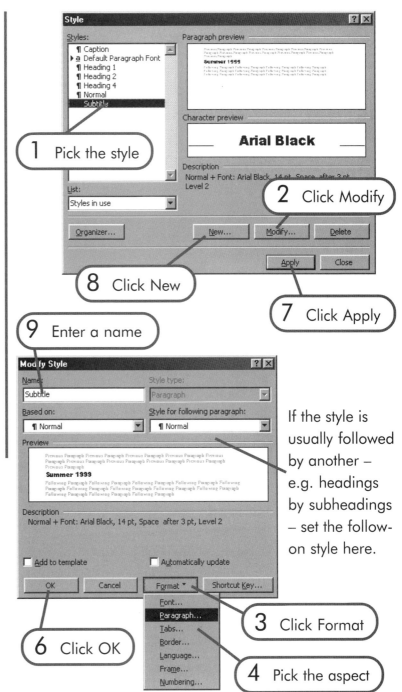

1 Pick the style

2 Click Modify

8 Click New

9 Enter a name

7 Click Apply

If the style is usually followed by another – e.g. headings by subheadings – set the follow-on style here.

6 Click OK

3 Click Format

4 Pick the aspect

59

Page Setup

If you are creating anything other than routine letters and memos, the Page Setup may well need changing.

Paper size

You will need to change the size if you are printing on envelopes or unusual paper, and should always check it when working from a template, which may have been set up for US paper size. Use this tab also to set the orientation – upright (Portrait) or sideways (Landscape).

Setting margins

Use the Margins tab to adjust the space around the printed area. Margins should not be too small – printers can't reach the very edge or the paper and you need some white space around any text. Sometimes a slight reduction of the margins will give you a better printout. There is little more irritating than a couple of odd lines of text or a tiny block of data on a separate sheet.

If you are printing both sides of the paper, book-style, tick the Mirror margins box. If they are to be ring-bound, widen the inner margin or set the gutter to allow for the hidden paper.

Paper source

This rarely needs attention. You might perhaps want to turn off the defaults so that you can manually feed in individual sheets of card or special paper, without emptying the paper tray.

Layout

This needs attention with large documents that have been divided into sections – you can set where each section starts – and where you have headers and footers, and don't want the same ones on every page.

Basic steps

1. Open the File menu and select Page Setup.

2. On the Paper Size tab, pick the size from the drop-down list.

3. Set the Orientation – *Portrait* or *Landscape.*

4. Go to the Margins tab. If required, turn on Mirror margins or 2 pages per sheet.

5. Use the ⬍ buttons to adjust the margins or enter new values.

6. On the Layout tab, set the Section start and Header and Footer options for large or multi-section documents, if appropriate.

7. Click ⬛ OK ⬛ when done.

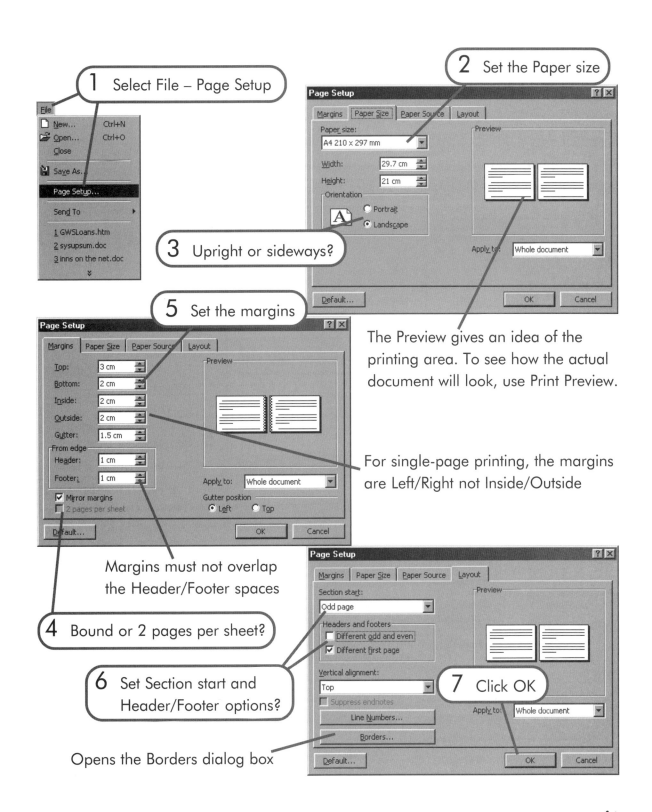

1 Select File – Page Setup

2 Set the Paper size

3 Upright or sideways?

The Preview gives an idea of the printing area. To see how the actual document will look, use Print Preview.

5 Set the margins

For single-page printing, the margins are Left/Right not Inside/Outside

Margins must not overlap the Header/Footer spaces

4 Bound or 2 pages per sheet?

6 Set Section start and Header/Footer options?

7 Click OK

Opens the Borders dialog box

Printing

Word documents are (normally) page-based from the start, leading to a simple transition from screen to paper. With a straightforward document of just a few pages, the 'instant print' approach should do nicely. If you have longer documents, or special printing requirements, the Print dialog box gives you good control of the output.

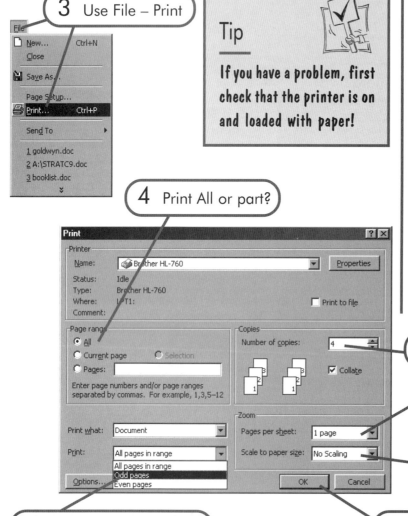

3   Use File – Print

4   Print All or part?

5   How many copies?

Small pages can be printed several to a sheet

Scale up or down to fit on different sized paper

6   Single or double-sided?

7   Click OK

Basic steps

❑ Instant print

1 Click 🖨.

❑ Controlled printing

2 If you only want to print part of a page, select the text first.

3 Open the File menu and select Print.

4 Set the range of pages to print.

5 Set the Copies number – turn on Collate to print multiple copies in sorted sets.

6 For double-sided printing, set the Print first to Odd pages then to Even pages.

7 Click OK.

Print Preview

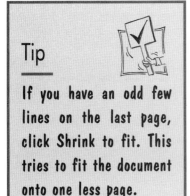

Tip

If you have an odd few lines on the last page, click Shrink to fit. This tries to fit the document onto one less page.

If you work in Print Layout view, you can see – as you create the document – how it will fit on paper. By dropping the Zoom level down to Whole page or Two pages, you can get a better impression of the overall layout of the document.

Print Preview lets you view more pages – as thumbnails – at a time, has a Zoom tool which you can use to jump between 100% and the preview size, and shows the headers and footers more clearly. When previewing, you can adjust font sizes, line spacing or the size and position of objects to get a better balanced page – all the normal menu commands are available and toolbars can be opened as needed.

Multiple pages   Ruler (on/ off)   Shrink to fit

One page   Zoom level   Full screen (removes frame and menu bar)

Print

Zoom (turn off to get editing pointer)

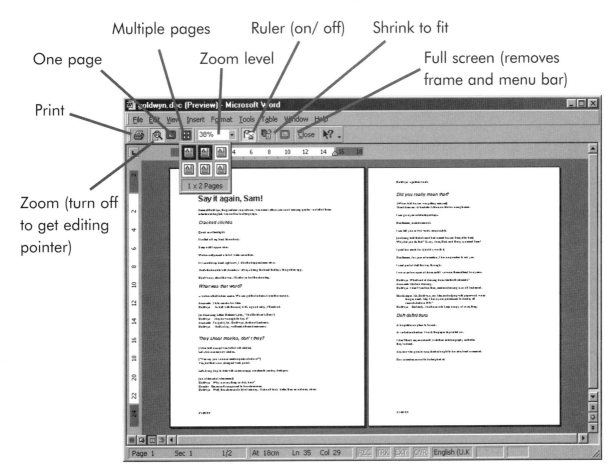

Summary

❏ Word can handle large and complex text-based jobs if required, but for straightforward work is exceptionally easy to use.

❏ Use the Normal view when creating a document, switching to the Web or Print layout views to check its layout, or to Outline view to reorganise paragraphs more easily.

❏ New documents can be started from scratch, or from a basic design set up by a template or wizard.

❏ Selected paragraphs can be set in columns.

❏ Headers and footers can be added to give fixed information on all pages.

❏ The use of Styles brings consistency to your formatting – and speeds up the job!

❏ If the output is anything other than A4 single sheets, use the Page Setup to define the layout.

❏ Use the File – Print routine if you need to control the output, and use the Print Preview to check the final layout before printing.

Tip

For more about Word 2000, read *Word 2000 Made Simple*, available in regular and business editions.

5 Excel

Introducing Excel

When spreadsheets first appeared, they were simply grids of cells into which text, numbers and formulae could be written. They have come a long way since then! Excel 2000 doesn't just perform your own calculations quickly and accurately, it also offers, amongst other things:

- a full range of functions and wizards for analysing data;

- database-style sorting and searching facilities;

- full control over the layout and appearance of text and numbers;

- easy-to-use but sophisticated graphing routines that can make underlying trends and patterns more visible.

The sheet that calculates the bills can also produce professional-looking invoices, record the sales and update the inventory.

Two layers

With a word-processed document, what you see is what you get. Spreadsheets are different. The data that you enter the sheet is not necessarily what you see on the screen or printed output. You (normally) see the the results of calculations, not the formulae; numbers can be displayed in different formats (see page 70); text may appear cropped short if it is too long to fit; and confidential data or calculations can be hidden if desired.

Entering and editing data

Entering data into a spreadsheet is significantly different from entering it into a word processor. Data is entered and edited through the Formula line, which is linked to the current cell. It displays whatever is in the cell at the moment, and anything typed into the Formula line is transferred to the cell after editing.

1 Point at the target cell and click on it to make it current.

❑ To enter data

2 Start to type – if you are entering a formula start with an = sign.

❑ To edit cell contents

3 Click in the Formula line, or press [F2] to start editing.

4 Use the [←] / [→] keys to move along the Formula line; [Backspace] or [Delete] to erase errors.

5 Click ☑ beside the Formula line, or press [Enter] when you have done. The data will appear in the cell.

Jargon

Current cell – the last one you clicked with the mouse. It is marked by a heavy border.

Cell reference – a Column letter/Row number combination that identifies a cell. Here the current cell is C3 (Column C, Row 3).

Range – a set of cells, which may be one or more full rows or columns, or a block somewhere in the middle of the sheet.

Formula line – the slot at the top. Its contents are transferred to the current cell when you press [Enter]. All data is entered into cells through this line.

Workbook – a set of sheets saved and used as one file. A formula in one sheet can draw in the data in any of the others.

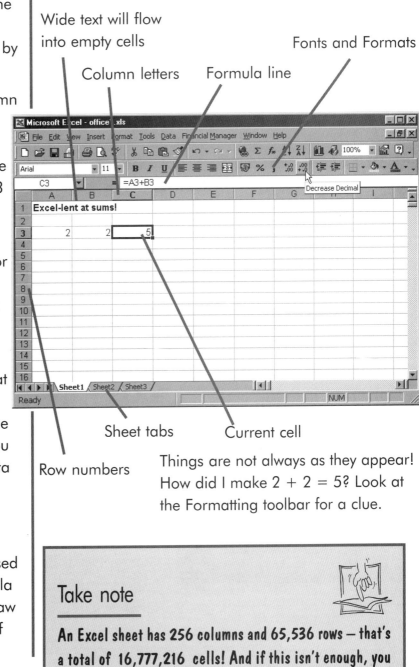

Wide text will flow into empty cells

Column letters

Formula line

Fonts and Formats

Sheet tabs

Current cell

Row numbers

Things are not always as they appear! How did I make 2 + 2 = 5? Look at the Formatting toolbar for a clue.

Take note

An Excel sheet has 256 columns and 65,536 rows – that's a total of 16,777,216 cells! And if this isn't enough, you can have as many sheets as you like in one workbook.

Selecting cells

Once you have selected a cell, or a range of cells, you can:

- apply a font style or alignment;
- add a border to some or all of its edges;
- erase its contents;
- use its references in a formula;
- move it to another position.

A range reference is made up of the cell references of the top left and bottom right corners. Most of the time you will be able to get the references by selecting the range with the mouse.

Block size – changes to reference
of top left cell when selected

1 Start here

2 Drag to the opposite corner

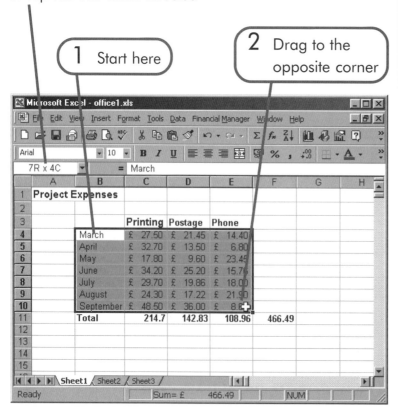

❏ To select a block

1 Point to the top left cell (or any corner).

2 Hold down the mouse button and drag the highlight over the block.

❏ To select a set of rows

3 Point to the row number at the top or bottom of the set.

4 Drag up or down over the numbers to high-light the rows you want.

Tip

In a selected range, all the cells will be shown in reverse colour, except for the first – the current cell. It's easy to think that this hasn't been selected. Don't be misled.

❏ To select a set of columns

5 Point to the letter of the first column.

6 Drag across the top of the columns to include the ones you want.

❏ To select all cells

7 Click in the top left corner, where the row and column headers meet.

❏ To select scattered cells

8 Select one, then hold down [Ctrl] key and click on the rest.

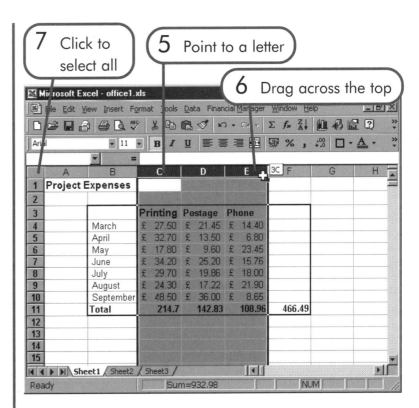

7 Click to select all

5 Point to a letter

6 Drag across the top

8 [Ctrl]-click to select

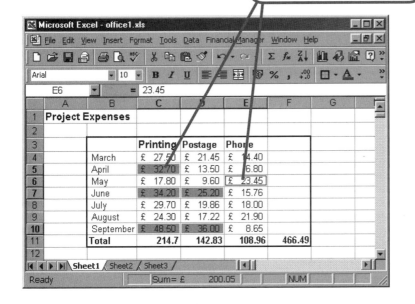

Take note

You can use the [Ctrl]-click technique to select cells for formatting or for use in a function, but a set of scattered cells cannot copied or moved.

69

Fonts and formats

Setting font types, styles and sizes for text is exactly the same here as it is in Word. Just select the cells and click a toolbar button or use **Format – Cells** and switch to the **Font** tab.

Number formats are a different matter. The way in which we write a number depends upon what it represents. If it is a money value, we would write a £ (or other currency sign) before and show two figures after the decimal point; with a large number, we would put commas every three digits to make it easier to read; if it is a percent, we place a % sign after it.

Excel knows about all this. It can display numbers in different formats, and can understand numbers that are written in different formats. Type in £12,345.67 and it will realise that the underlying number is 12345.67, and also that you want to display it as currency. Type in 50% and it will store it as 0.5, while showing 50% on screen. Type in 0181-123 4567 and it will not be fooled into thinking it's a sum – this gets treated as text. Try it and see for yourself.

Basic steps

1 Select the range of cells to be formatted.

2 From the Format menu select Cells…

3 On the Number tab, select a format from the Category list.

4 Set the number of decimal places.

5 With the *Number* and *Currency* formats, set the Negative numbers style.

6 With *Currency*, pick a Symbol if necessary.

7 Click [OK].

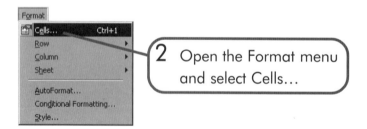

2 Open the Format menu and select Cells…

Take note

The Currency, Comma and Percent formats can be set from the Formatting toolbar buttons.

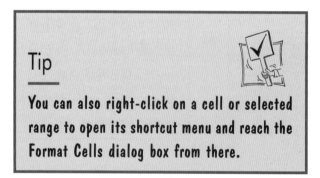

Tip

You can also right-click on a cell or selected range to open its shortcut menu and reach the Format Cells dialog box from there.

General displays most values in *Number* format, large ones in *Exponential.*

Number as 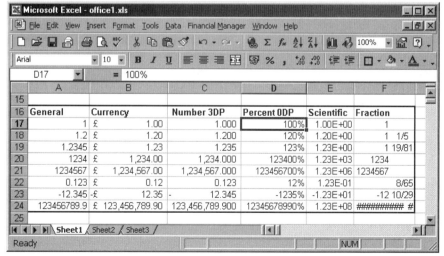, with commas every 3 digits, and 2 decimal places.

Currency 🖳 as Number, with a currency sign (e.g. £) at the front.

Percent % multiplies the value by 100 and adds % at the end.

Fractions to nearest common fraction or up to 3 digit accuracy.

Scientific for very large or small numbers.

Text treats digits as text.

If you see "######" increase the column width to display the number properly

3 Choose a format

4 Set the decimal places

Format Cells

Number | Alignment | Font | Border | Patterns | Protection

Category:
General
Number
Currency
Accounting
Date
Time
Percentage
Fraction
Scientific
Text
Special
Custom

Sample
March

Decimal places: 2

Symbol:
£

Negative numbers:
-£1,234.10
£1,234.10
-£1,234.10
-£1,234.10

6 Change symbol?

Currency formats are used for general monetary values. Use Accounting formats to align decimal points in a column.

5 Negative in red?

OK   Cancel

7 Click OK

A small selection of the number formats that Excel can handle. The number of decimal places can be set in any format. With Currency and Number formats, you can have negative numbers shown in red.

Microsoft Excel - office1.xls

File Edit View Insert Format Tools Data Financial Manager Window Help

Arial ... 10 ... **B** *I* U ... 🗐 % , ... 🗀 ...

D17 = 100%

	A	B	C	D	E	F
15						
16	General	Currency	Number 3DP	Percent 0DP	Scientific	Fraction
17	1	£ 1.00	1.000	100%	1.00E+00	1
18	1.2	£ 1.20	1.200	120%	1.20E+00	1 1/5
19	1.2345	£ 1.23	1.235	123%	1.23E+00	1 19/81
20	1234	£ 1,234.00	1,234.000	123400%	1.23E+03	1234
21	1234567	£ 1,234,567.00	1,234,567.000	123456700%	1.23E+06	1234567
22	0.123	£ 0.12	0.123	12%	1.23E-01	8/65
23	-12.345	-£ 12.35	- 12.345	-1235%	-1.23E+01	-12 10/29
24	123456789.9	£ 123,456,789.90	123,456,789.900	12345678990%	1.23E+08	########## #
25						

Sheet1 / Sheet2 / Sheet3 /

Ready   NUM

Alignment

In Excel, all text must be written into cells, and this can create some problems. If you have more text than will fit into the cell, it will be cut short if there is something in the cell to its right. The simple solution – widening the column – can create its own problems as the extra wide column may mess up the display in the rows below or above.

A spreadsheet is essentially about numbers, so ensuring that the numbers are displayed clearly must be the prime aim. Any text should then be fitted as neatly as possible around that number display. Excel offers a number of solutions:

● **Wrap text**: text runs on two or more lines within the cell.

● **Shrink to fit**: text is reduced in size until it fits – handy for squeezing the odd extra letter into the cell.

● **Merge cells**: joins two or more cells together, allowing text in the leftmost to flow right across.

● **Orientation**: allows text to be displayed on the slant so that it takes up less width.

● **Center across selection**: (⊞ on the Formatting toolbar) centres the text in the leftmost cell across a set of cells.

These are all available on the **Alignment** tab of the **Format Cells** dialog box. You will also find there the normal horizontal alignment options – Left, Center, Right and Justify – plus settings for the *vertical* alignment – Bottom, Center, Top, Justify.

Most of the options are straightforward – select the cells, go to the Alignment tab and set the options. The basic steps just cover the two trickier ones.

Basic steps

❑ Setting Orientation

1 Select the cells.

2 From the Format menu select Cells...

3 Switch to the Alignment tab.

4 Drag the red marker around the arc to set the angle.

5 Click [OK].

❑ Center across selection

6 Type the text into the leftmost cell of the set.

7 Select the set of cells.

8 Click ▦.

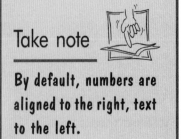

Take note
_____
By default, numbers are aligned to the right, text to the left.

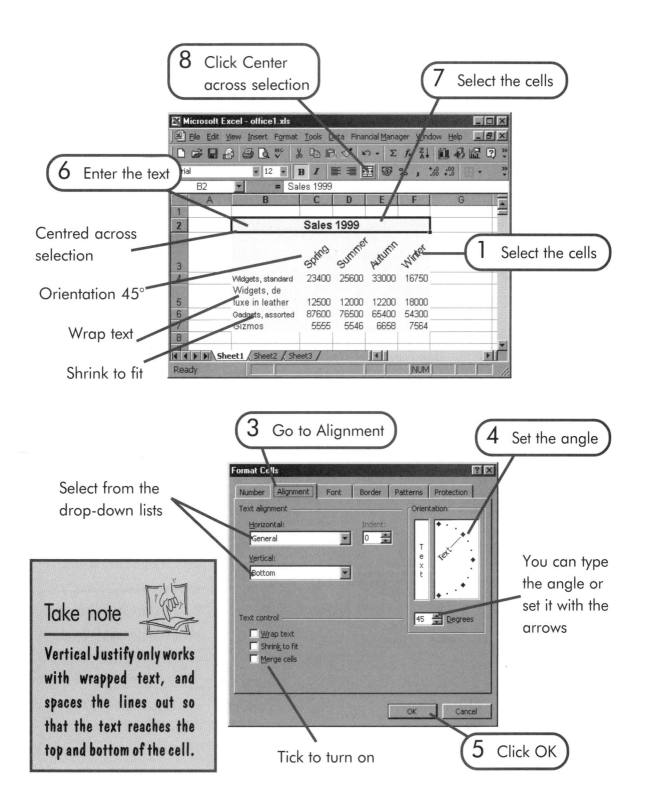

8 Click Center across selection

7 Select the cells

6 Enter the text

Centred across selection

Orientation 45°

Wrap text

Shrink to fit

1 Select the cells

3 Go to Alignment

4 Set the angle

Select from the drop-down lists

You can type the angle or set it with the arrows

Take note

Vertical Justify only works with wrapped text, and spaces the lines out so that the text reaches the top and bottom of the cell.

Tick to turn on

5 Click OK

Autoformats

Excel's Autoformats, like Word's, offer an instant design solution for common situations. They are all based on headed tables or lists, but with 17 alternatives to choose from, you should find something there to suit most of your needs. The formatting includes that of the numbers, the style of text and the size of the rows and columns as well as shading and borders. If you have some formatting already in place, e.g. the number display, you can choose not to overwrite it with the AutoFormat.

Colours and shades are best avoided if you are not using a colour printer, as they will be printed in grey and could be darker than you expect – making text difficult to read.

1 Select the table or list to be formatted, including its headers and totals.

2 Open the Format menu and select AutoFormat...

3 Pick a format.

4 If there are aspects you do not want to apply, click Options... and clear the checkbox by the unwanted options.

5 Click OK .

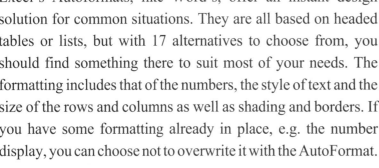

2 Use Format – AutoFormat...

3 Select a format

5 Click OK

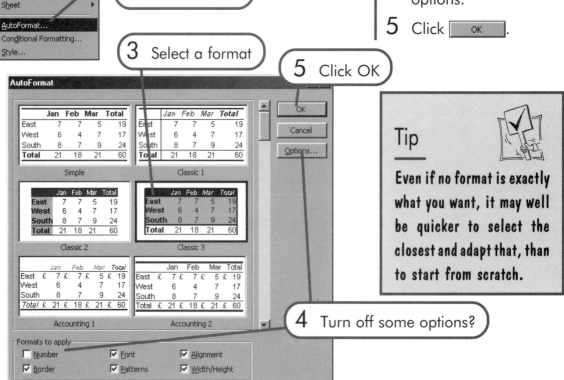

4 Turn off some options?

Tip

Even if no format is exactly what you want, it may well be quicker to select the closest and adapt that, than to start from scratch.

Basic steps

Writing formulae

❑ **To total a range**

1 Click on the cell below the column (or to the right of the row).

2 Click the Σ Autosum button.

3 You will see that the column (or row) is highlighted, and that there is =SUM(*range*) in the formula line.

4 If the range covers the right cells, click ☑ or press [Enter] to accept the formula.

You won't get far with a spreadsheet without writing formulae, but at least Excel makes it a fairly painless business. If you just want to total a column or row of figures, it only takes a click of a button with **Autosum**. Other calculations take a little more effort, but point and click references, and readily-accessible lists of functions simplify the process and reduce the chance of errors.

A formula starts with the = sign and can contain a mixture of cell or range references, numbers, text and functions, joined by operators. These include the arithmetic symbols / (divide) * (multiply) + (add) - (subtract) ^ (power) and a few others.

Examples of simple formulae:

= 4 * C1   4 times the contents of cell C1

= B3+B4   the value in B3 added to that in B4

=SUM(A5:A12) the sum of the values in cells A5 to A12.

References can be typed into the formula line, or pulled in by clicking on a cell or highlighting a range.

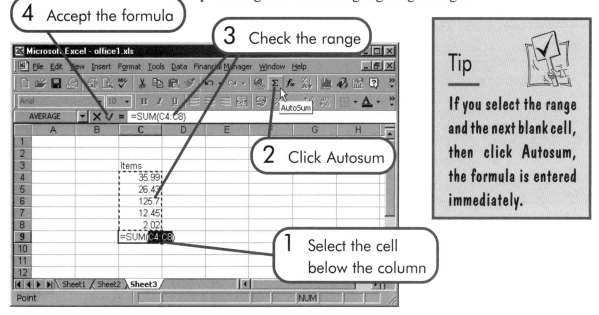

4 Accept the formula

3 Check the range

2 Click Autosum

1 Select the cell below the column

Tip

If you select the range and the next blank cell, then click Autosum, the formula is entered immediately.

Mathematical formulae

The following operators can be used in Excel formulae:

+	Addition	–	Subtraction
*	Multiplication	/	Division
^	raise to the power	()	brackets

Where there are several operators in a formula, the normal rules of precedence are followed – power, then multiplication/division, and finally addition/subtraction. Operations in brackets are performed first. e.g. $4 * 3 + 2 = 14$, but $4 * (3 + 2) = 20$.

- ❏ To write a formula
- 1 Click on the cell where the formula is to go.
- 2 Type '='.
- 3 Type the number, or point and click to get a cell reference.
- 4 Type an operator.
- 5 Type the next number, or select the next reference.
- 6 Repeat steps 4 and 5, as necessary, to complete the formula.
- 7 Click ☑ or press [Enter].

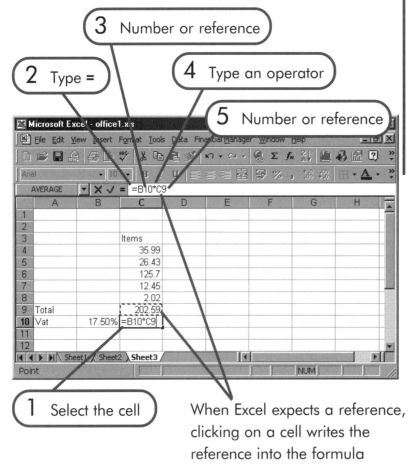

3 Number or reference

2 Type =

4 Type an operator

5 Number or reference

1 Select the cell

When Excel expects a reference, clicking on a cell writes the reference into the formula

Tip

If a cell displays the formula, not its result, there is an error in it. Select the cell and press [F2] to edit it.

Basic steps

❏ To name a range

1 Select the cell or the range.

2 Open the Insert menu and select Name then Define...

3 An adjacent text item may be suggested as the name – edit it or type a new name.

4 Click ☐ OK ☐.

❏ To remove a name

5 Open the Define Name... dialog box.

6 Highlight the name and click ☐ Delete ☐.

Cell and range references are hard to remember, and if you reorganise the layout of the spreadsheet, you may have to learn them all again. To make life simpler, Excel allows you to give meaningful names to cells and ranges. Use them. They will make your formulae more readable, and if you want to transfer data into a word processed document, you can only do this with named ranges.

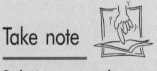

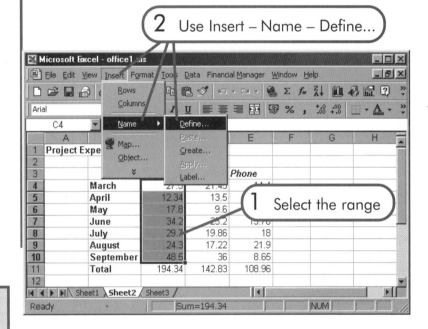

2 Use Insert – Name – Define...

1 Select the range

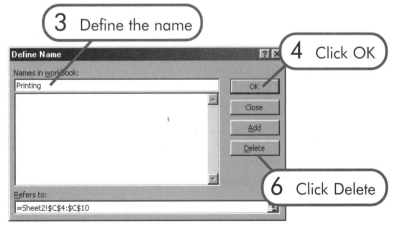

3 Define the name

4 Click OK

6 Click Delete

Take note

Deleting a name does not affect anything else. The contents of the cells will be untouched, and references will replace any names that were used in formulae.

Functions

A function takes one or more number or text values, performs some kind of process on them and gives a new value in return. It may be a simple process, as with SUM, which adds up a range of numbers. It may be a familiar one such as SIN, which gives the sine of an angle. It may be a complex process that you wouldn't meet anywhere except on a spreadsheet. PMT, for example, will give you the regular repayment on a mortgage. There is no room here to look at these functions properly, but what we can do is cover the basics of how to use them.

Almost all functions take one or more -. These can be values, cell or range references or other functions. They are written in brackets, after the function name, e.g. INT(3.141) – which converts a value to an integer – or COUNT(B1:B9,D1:D9) – which finds how many cells in the two ranges contain values.

If you know how a function works and what sort of arguments it needs, you can type it into the Formula line. In general, it is simpler to use the function list and the Paste Function dialog box, and be guided through the construction of the function.

Basic steps

1 Select the cell into which the formula should go.

2 Type '='.

3 Drop down the function list.

4 If you can see the one you want, select it.

Otherwise

5 Click More Functions...

6 Select a category, then a function and click OK.

7 To select a cell or range, click 🔳 to shrink the function panel.

8 Select the cell/range to get the reference and click 🔳 to reopen the panel.

9 Enter other references or values as required and click OK.

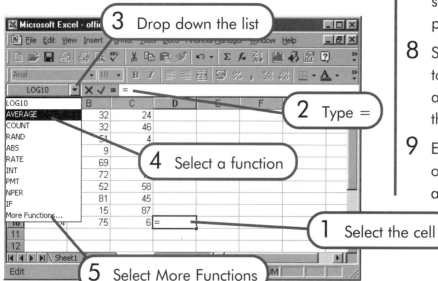

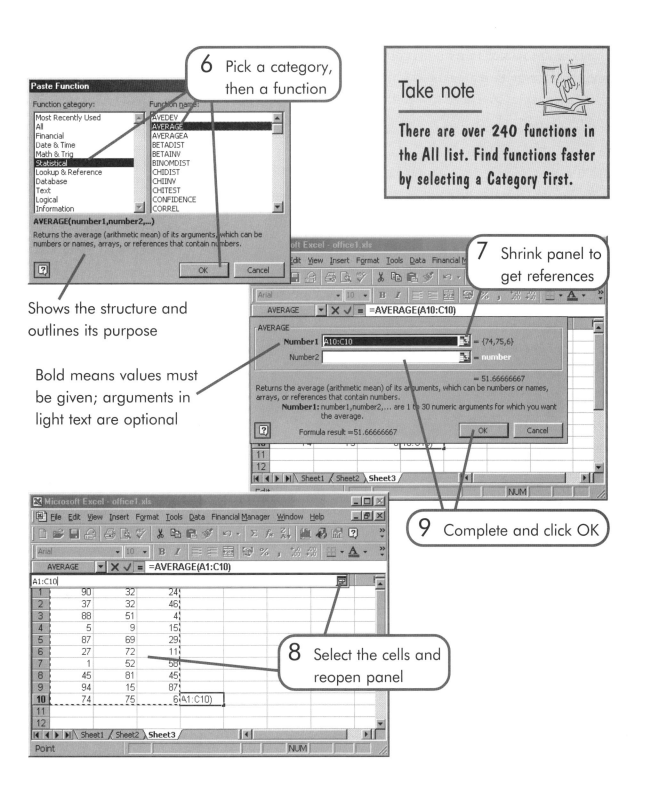

6 Pick a category, then a function

Paste Function

Function category:
- Most Recently Used
- All
- Financial
- Date & Time
- Math & Trig
- **Statistical**
- Lookup & Reference
- Database
- Text
- Logical
- Information

Function name:
- AVEDEV
- AVERAGE
- AVERAGEA
- BETADIST
- BETAINV
- BINOMDIST
- CHIDIST
- CHIINV
- CHITEST
- CONFIDENCE
- CORREL

AVERAGE(number1,number2,...)

Returns the average (arithmetic mean) of its arguments, which can be numbers or names, arrays, or references that contain numbers.

OK   Cancel

Take note

There are over 240 functions in the All list. Find functions faster by selecting a Category first.

Shows the structure and outlines its purpose

Bold means values must be given; arguments in light text are optional

7 Shrink panel to get references

Microsoft Excel - office1.xls

Edit View Insert Format Tools Data Financial M...

Arial   10   B I

AVERAGE   = =AVERAGE(A10:C10)

AVERAGE

Number1 A10:C10   = {74,75,6}

Number2   = number

= 51.66666667

Returns the average (arithmetic mean) of its arguments, which can be numbers or names, arrays, or references that contain numbers.

Number1: number1,number2,... are 1 to 30 numeric arguments for which you want the average.

Formula result =51.66666667   OK   Cancel

Sheet1 / Sheet2 \ Sheet3 /

9 Complete and click OK

Microsoft Excel - office1.xls

File Edit View Insert Format Tools Data Financial Manager Window Help

Arial   10   B I   %   A

AVERAGE   X √ = =AVERAGE(A1:C10)

A1:C10

1	90	32	24
2	37	32	46
3	88	51	4
4	5	9	15
5	87	69	29
6	27	72	11
7	1	52	58
8	45	81	45
9	94	15	87
10	74	75	6 A1:C10)
11			
12			

Sheet1 / Sheet2 \ Sheet3 /

Point   NUM

8 Select the cells and reopen panel

Lookup functions

The Lookup functions are worth exploration – they can be really useful, and in getting to grips with these you will master most of the techniques you need for working with other functions.

A Lookup function will scan through a list of items in a table, to find a key item, then pick a value out of the corresponding place in another column within the table. The example shows two Lookup formulae being used on a simple price and stock list. When an item's name is typed into a key cell, the functions scan the list and pick out its price and stock level.

There are two similar functions.

● **HLOOKUP** works with tables where the index values are written across the top of the table;

● **VLOOKUP** expects the index values to be down the left side of the table.

Basic steps

❑ To use VLOOKUP

1 Create a table of data, with index values on the left.

2 Pick a cell into which you will write the key value and type in something which is in the table. This will test the formula.

3 Select the cell which will hold the formula and type '='.

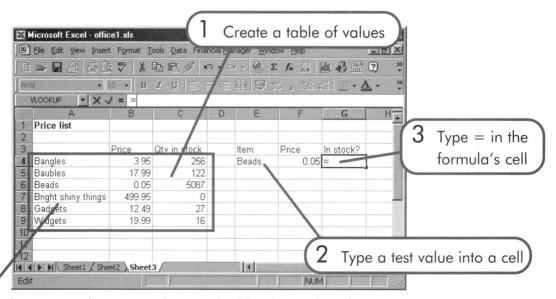

The index items – the ones to be matched by the Lookup function – must be in the first column and in ascending order. The values to be looked up are in columns to its right.

4 Drop down the function list and select More Functions.

5 Open the Lookup and Reference category, and select VLOOKUP.

6 For the *Lookup_value*, select or enter the reference of the cell containing your key value.

7 Click into *Table_array* and select the range that covers the table.

8 For *Col_index_num*, type 2 to get values from the first column to the right of the index values, or 3 to get values from the second column.

9 Click [OK].

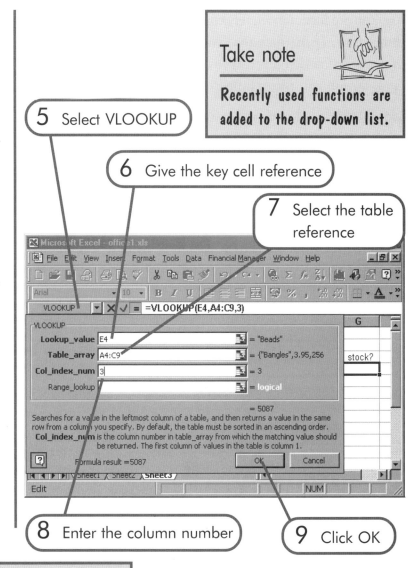

Take note

Recently used functions are added to the drop-down list.

5 Select VLOOKUP

6 Give the key cell reference

7 Select the table reference

Microsoft Excel - office1.xls

File Edit View Insert Format Tools Data Financial Manager Window Help

VLOOKUP = =VLOOKUP(E4,A4:C9,3)

VLOOKUP
Lookup_value E4 = "Beads"
Table_array A4:C9 = {"Bangles",3.95,256}
Col_index_num 3 = 3
Range_lookup = logical

= 5087

Searches for a value in the leftmost column of a table, and then returns a value in the same row from a column you specify. By default, the table must be sorted in an ascending order.
Col_index_num is the column number in table_array from which the matching value should be returned. The first column of values in the table is column 1.

Formula result =5087   Ok   Cancel

Sheet1 / Sheet2 \Sheet3 /

Edit   NUM

G

stock?

8 Enter the column number

9 Click OK

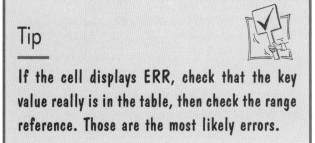

Tip

If the cell displays ERR, check that the key value really is in the table, then check the range reference. Those are the most likely errors.

Charts

You can produce some lovely charts with Excel – and with very little effort. If the data that you want to chart is organised properly in the first place, then charting is a breeze – and if it isn't, the job will take a little longer, but is still not difficult.

Ideally, the data should be in a continuous block – no unwanted rows or columns in the middle – with headings above and to the side. If the data is in rows, i.e. each row is displayed as a line on a graph or a set of bars on a chart, then the top headings will be used to label the bottom axis of the chart, and the side headings will identify the rows in the legend. Where the data is in columns, the headings will be used the other way round.

With data in this form, you can simply run the Chart Wizard, which will collect a few choices from you and create the graph.

Basic steps

1 Select the data to be charted, along with the relevant headers.

2 Click ▥ the Chart Wizard tool.

3 Select a Chart Type, then a sub-type, or a Custom Type and click Next > .

4 Check the Data range – click ▥ if you need to redefine the range – and the Series in Rows/Columns setting. Click Next > .

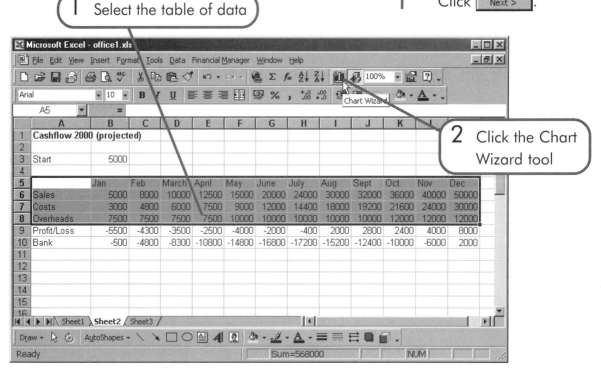

1 Select the table of data

2 Click the Chart Wizard tool

5 Enter the Chart title and Axis labels, if wanted.

6 Explore the options on the other tabs.

cont...

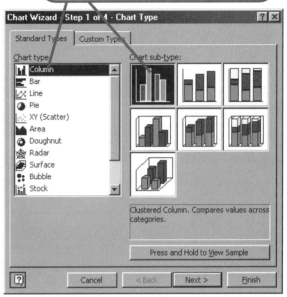

3 Select the type and sub-type

There are 14 types and 70 sub-types and 20 custom types to choose from!

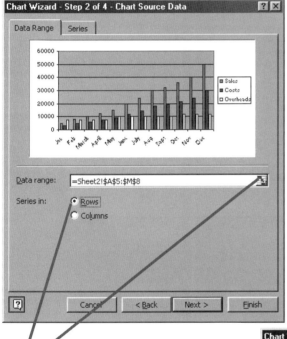

6 Set other options

These all control the display of items around the main chart

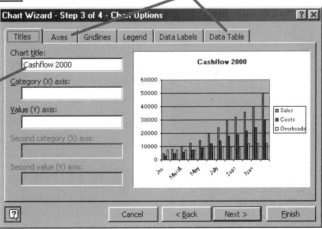

4 Set the range and Series in value

5 Enter the titles

Titles are not necessary on the axes if their meaning is obvious – e.g. 'time' or 'value'

cont...

7 Select where the chart is to go – as a new sheet or as an object in an existing sheet.

8 Click [Finish].

9 If the chart is placed in a sheet, the Wizard will drop it into the middle – drag it into place and resize it.

⑦ Where do you want it?

⑧ Click Finish

⑨ Move and resize as needed

Drag a handle to resize

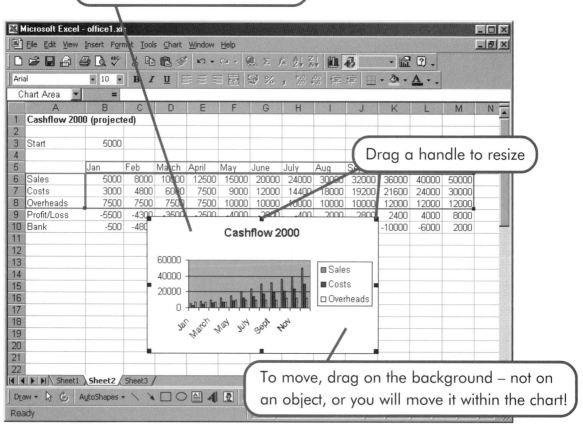

To move, drag on the background – not on an object, or you will move it within the chart!

Basic steps

1 Right-click on a bar in the series.

2 Select Chart Type… and set it to Line – only that series will be affected.

3 Right-click on the line and select a Format Data Series…

4 To plot the line series against the right-hand axis, go to the Axis tab and select Secondary axis.

Legend dragged to a new position

Formatting charts

Almost every aspect of a chart can be formatted individually to give you just the effect you want – right-click on any object to see the options on its short menu. Fonts, colours, line styles and similar are formatted as elsewhere in Office. A few options are unique to graphs. Here, for example is how to display one series as a line within a bar chart, with its own axis.

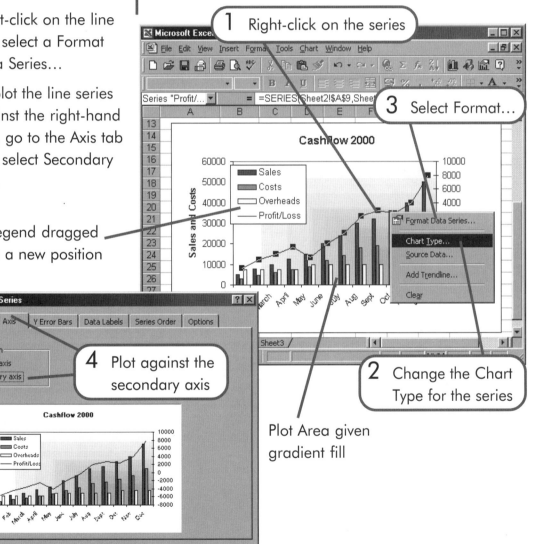

1 Right-click on the series

3 Select Format…

2 Change the Chart Type for the series

4 Plot against the secondary axis

Plot Area given gradient fill

Printing

Printing is not as straightforward in Excel as in some applications. Spreadsheets are of indefinite size and highly variable layout, so the printout may fit on a single page or be spread across many. To get a good-looking printout you may have to adjust the orientation of the paper, the scale of the print and other aspects.

If the sheet will need more than one page, use the **Page Setup** panel to define how it will be split up for printing and to add headers/footers and other optional extras. Use the Print Preview to check that your setup works, before you commit it to paper.

Normally, the whole active area, i.e. where the cells contain data, will be printed.

Basic steps

1 Select the cells if you only want to print part of the active sheet.

2 From the File menu select Page Setup....

3 On the Page tab, set the Orientation and Scaling – reduce large sheets or set the Fit to pages options.

4 On the Sheet tab, define the Print area if needed, and set the Rows and Columns to repeat for labels on multi-page printing.

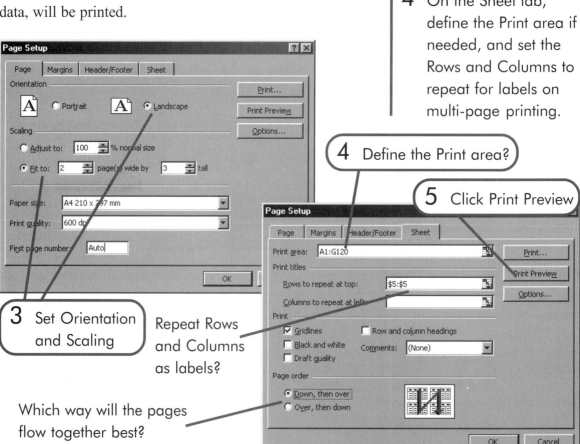

3 Set Orientation and Scaling

Repeat Rows and Columns as labels?

Which way will the pages flow together best?

4 Define the Print area?

5 Click Print Preview

5 Click [Print Preview].

6 Check the preview. If it needs adjusting, click [Setup...] to return to the Page Setup.

7 Click [Print...].

8 Set the Print range, Number of copies and other options as usual.

9 Click [OK].

Check the Fit to page and Page order settings before entering the Print range

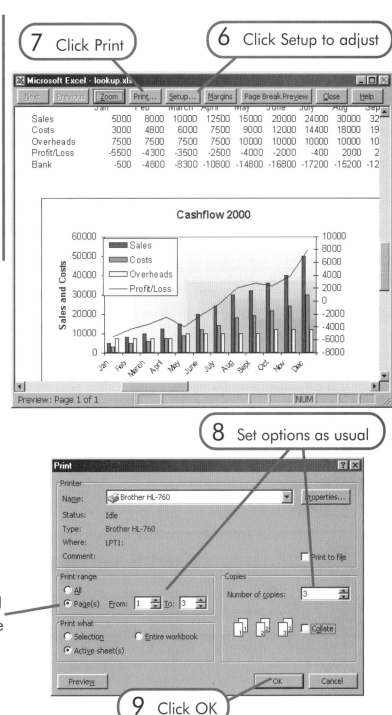

⑦ Click Print

⑥ Click Setup to adjust

⑧ Set options as usual

⑨ Click OK

Summary

- An Excel sheet is a grid of cells, each identified by its row and column reference.

- A cell's contents and its screen display may differ.

- Rows and columns can be selected by their header numbers and letters; blocks are selected by dragging from one corner to the opposite one.

- The appearance of the sheet can be enhanced by the use of fonts, alignments, borders and shading.

- Numbers can be displayed in different formats.

- The alignment options give you many ways to fit text within and across cells.

- The Autoformat options provide a quick way to give a professional finish to tables.

- Formulae all start with = and may include a mixture of text and number values, cell and range reference and functions.

- There is a wide range of functions, organised into several categories. They are easily accessed through the Insert Function dialog box.

- The Lookup functions allow you to write formulae that will extract information from a table.

- You can easily produce attractive and informative charts from tables of data.

- Printing normally needs planning as a spreadsheet may well not fit neatly onto sheets of paper.

Tip

For more about Excel 2000, read *Excel 2000 Made Simple*, available in regular and business editions.

6 Powerpoint

Introducing PowerPoint

PowerPoint is used for producing presentations, to be viewed as overhead projections, directly on a computer, through a Web browser or even as a proper slide show.

A presentation may contain:

- **text**, typically in bullet points, though larger blocks of text can be written;

- **images** – clip art, scanned pictures, photographs and drawings – which may be essential illustrations or just to brighten things up;

- **video and sound clips**, and even recorded commentary synchronised with the presentations;

- **graphs, organisation charts** and embedded objects from other applications.

All of these can be formatted in the usual ways, and displayed on a coloured, patterned or picture background.

The central part of any presentation is a set of 'slides'. At the simplest, these will be displayed, in full, one after the other, but if you want more, you can have animated transitions between slides, build slide displays by flying in their components one by one or using other visual effects, and let the audience pick its own path through the set.

Each slide can be accompanied by notes, which can be printed out for the presenter's benefit, or incorporated into handouts for the audience. The handouts can be anything from simple reminders, with the slides printed in miniature 9 to a page, or full course notes – you can even use PowerPoint in the same way as you would use Word, to produce full pages of text and images.

Take note

This chapter is just a quick introduction to the essentials of PowerPoint. Chapters 7 and 8 will tell you more about working with text, images and other objects, but if you need to get deeper into Power-Point, try *PowerPoint 2000 Made Simple.*

The PowerPoint window

This has five main views, though the same elements are found
– in different proportions – in three of the four working views.

- **Normal view** is best for general work, but switch to **Outline** when you want to concentrate on the text and **Slide view** for working on the layout or inserted objects.

- Use **Slide Sorter view** for a quick overview of the material and to reorganise the order.

- Use **Slide Show view** to see the presentation in action.

Outline pane, bigger in Outline view   Standard toolbar   Slide pane, bigger in Slide view

Formatting toolbar

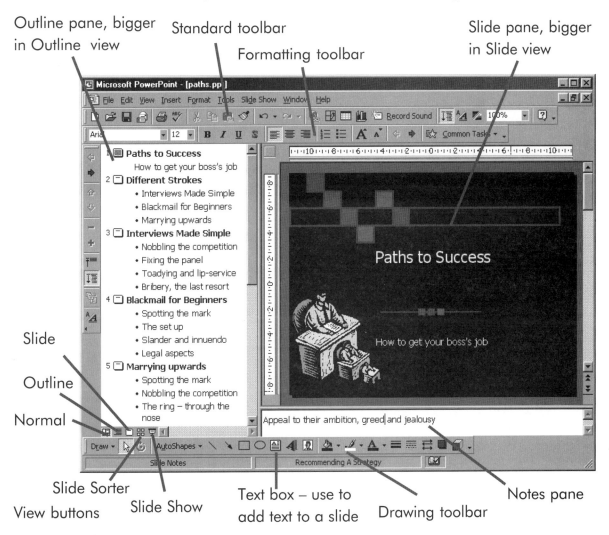

Slide

Outline

Normal

Slide Sorter

View buttons   Slide Show   Text box – use to add text to a slide   Drawing toolbar   Notes pane

New presentation

PowerPoint offers three approaches to creating a presentation.

- **Blank presentation** leaves it entirely up to you;

- **Design Templates** have the background and the font styles, sizes and colours set up for you;

- **AutoContent Wizard** and **Presentation Templates** have the design elements in place, plus whole structure of the presentation, with suggested content.

Here's how to start from a Design Template.

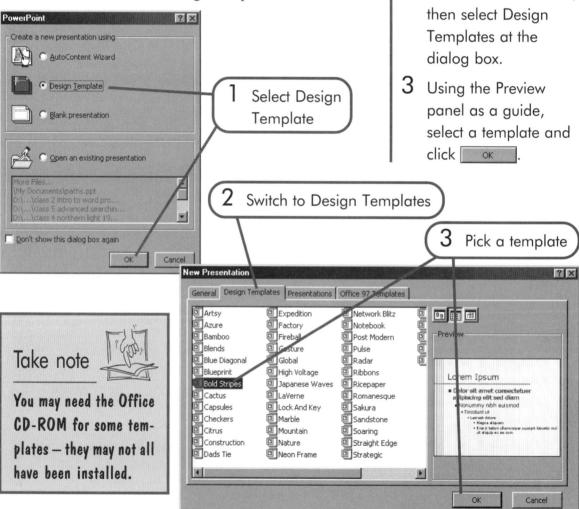

1 Select Design Template

2 Switch to Design Templates

3 Pick a template

Take note

You may need the Office CD-ROM for some templates — they may not all have been installed.

1 When you first start PowerPoint, select Design Template and click OK.

Or

2 If PowerPoint is running, open the File menu and select New, then select Design Templates at the dialog box.

3 Using the Preview panel as a guide, select a template and click OK.

4 At the New Slide
dialog box, select a
layout for your first
slide and click
OK .

5 Replace the *Click to
add text* prompts with
your own text – just
click on them and they
disappear. Likewise,
double-click in any
object frame to add
an object of that type.

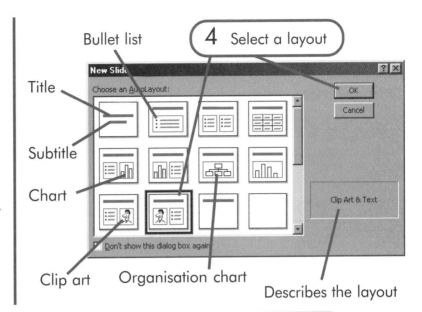

Title

Subtitle

Chart

Clip art

Bullet list

4 Select a layout

Organisation chart

Describes the layout

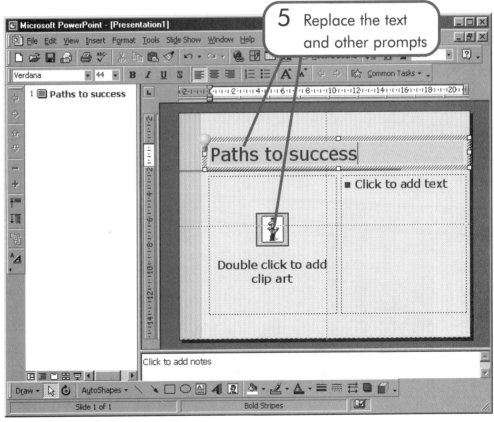

5 Replace the text
and other prompts

Off-the-shelf presentations

There are 24 of these, which you can reach either through the Presentations tab of the New Presentation dialog box or the AutoContent Wizard – the Wizard simply collects a little information before opening.

Basic steps

❑ Using the Wizard

1 Select AutoContent Wizard at startup or from the General tab of the New Presentation dialog box.

2 Select the type – the Carnegie Coach ones are all 'motivational'.

3 Select the style.

4 In the options, enter the title and footer.

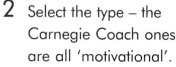

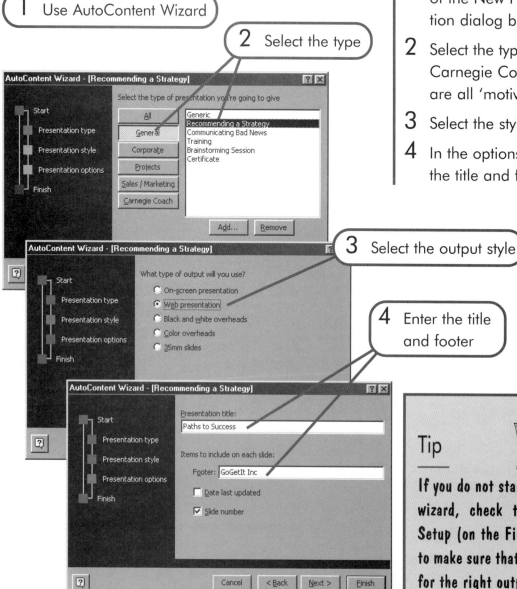

Tip

If you do not start from a wizard, check the Page Setup (on the File menu) to make sure that it is set for the right output type.

94

❑ The Presentations tab

5 Select Design Templates at startup or use File – New.

6 Open the Presentations tab of the New Presentation dialog box.

7 Select a presentation and click OK.

❑ Customising

8 Switch to Outline view.

9 Replace the titles and other text.

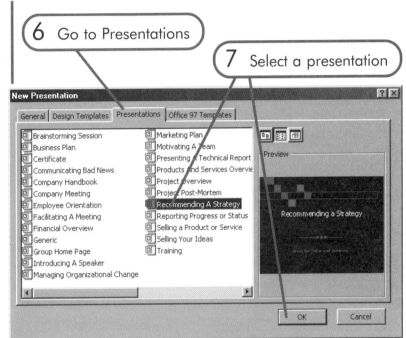

6 Go to Presentations

7 Select a presentation

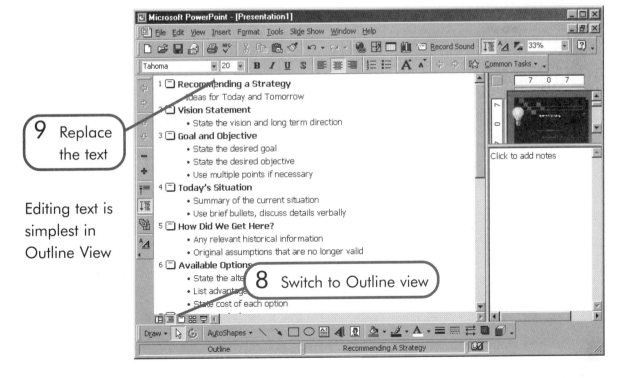

9 Replace the text

Editing text is simplest in Outline View

8 Switch to Outline view

Text on slides

Once you have got text onto a slide, it can be edited and formatted in exactly the same way as text in Word – the difference is in how you get the text there in the first place. You cannot simply type onto a slide, instead you must insert a text box and type into there. Don't worry too much about placing a new box accurately – it can be moved or resized freely, you can get your text exactly where and how you want it afterwards.

Basic steps

1 Open the Insert menu and select Text box.

Or

2 Click ▤ on the Drawing toolbar.

3 Click where you want one corner of the box and drag an outline.

4 Type your text, then format it as normal.

5 Drag the outline to move, or a handle to resize the text box.

Tip

See Chapter 7 for how to format text.

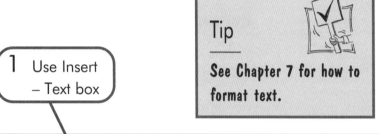

1 Use Insert – Text box

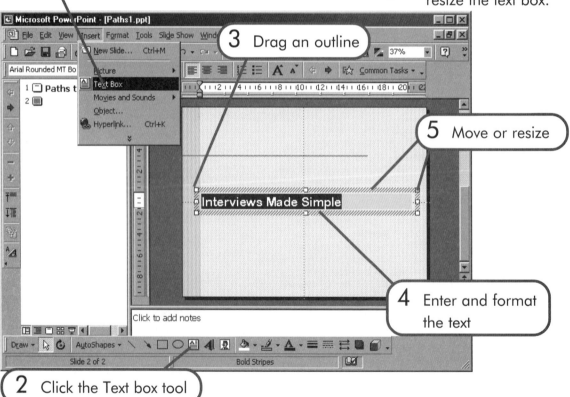

3 Drag an outline

5 Move or resize

4 Enter and format the text

2 Click the Text box tool

Basic steps

Pictures and other objects

❑ Inserting Objects

1 Double-click the Object icon in a slide.

Or

2 Open the Insert menu and select Object.

3 To create a new object, select the Object type from the list and click ` OK `.

4 To use an existing object, select Create from file, then browse for the file.

5 What happens next depend entirely on the object.

If you want pictures or other objects on a slide, use the Insert menu options, or – the easy way – start from a new slide containing the right kind of object placeholder (a frame with a link to the object type). Just double-click on the icon and you are into its insert routine.

 Clip art – see page 127

 Graph 2000 – see page 144

 Media clip (Sound and Motion) – see page 130

 Object – see also page 154

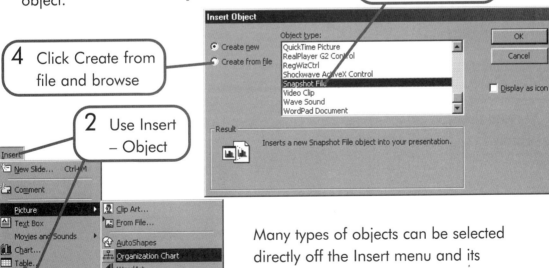 Organization Chart – see next page

Most of these are covered elsewhere in this book. We'll look briefly at Objects and Organization Charts here.

3 Select the type

4 Click Create from file and browse

2 Use Insert – Object

Many types of objects can be selected directly off the Insert menu and its submenus – have a look at what's there

Organization Chart

You can insert organization charts into any Office document, but they are more closely linked to PowerPoint, where you will find them ready-formatted.

The concept is simple. A chart consists of boxes containing the name, title and comments for each person. They can be linked to each other in different ways to indicate the nature of the relationship. Starting from the basic boss + three underlings, you can add boxes for five types of relationships to build a chart for your organisation.

Basic steps

1 Double-click on 🔳 to get into the chart.

2 Replace the names and title, and type comments if wanted.

❑ To add a box

3 Click the tool for the relationship.

4 Click the box that the new one relates to.

❑ To delete a box

5 Click on it and press [Delete].

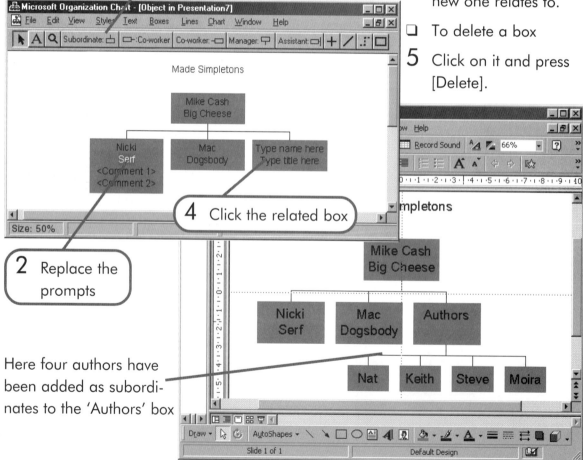

3 Select the relationship

4 Click the related box

2 Replace the prompts

Here four authors have been added as subordinates to the 'Authors' box

98

Basic steps

1 Switch to Slide Sorter view.

2 Select the slide to be moved.

3 Drag across the screen – a line will show where the slide will be placed.

4 Release the mouse button.

The main purpose of this view is – of course – for sorting slides, but it can also be useful to give you an overview of the whole set. Are they all too much the same? With shorter presentations, consistency can be a good thing, but too much of the same is something else! Are the illustrations, if any, spaced to (re)capture your audience's attention? You can, and should, test your presentation to check just these things, but at an early stage, Slide Sorter view gives you a quick way to see it all.

Reorganising the slide is simple.

Tip

You can also move slides by dragging the slide icons in the Outline pane — but the effects are more visible in Slide Sorter view.

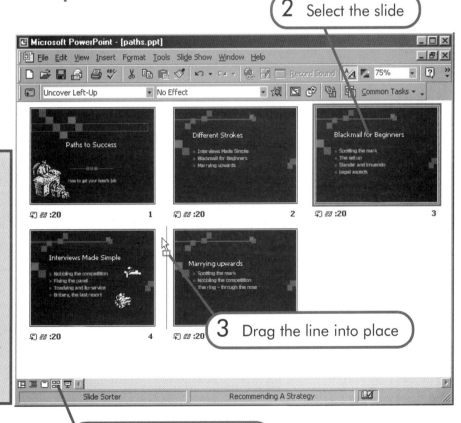

2 Select the slide

3 Drag the line into place

1 Go to Slide Sorter view

Transition and Animation

Slide transition controls how the show progresses from one slide to another. You can specify:

- How a slide becomes visible – selecting from a wide range of covering/uncovering, dissolves, venetian blind, checkerboards and other effects.

- The speed of the transition.

- Accompanying sound effects – go easy on these, they can put the audience off if overdone.

- When the new slide should appear – after a set time or on a mouse click.

If none are set, then the presenter will have to run the show manually, using the keyboard or mouse, and slides will simply come on screen, replacing the previous one.

Basic steps

1 Open the Slide Show menu and select Slide Transition...

2 Select an Effect.

3 Set the speed.

4 Turn on Automatically after and set the timing, if wanted.

5 Pick a Sound if useful.

6 Click [Apply] to apply the transition to the current slide, or [Apply to All] to apply it to the whole show.

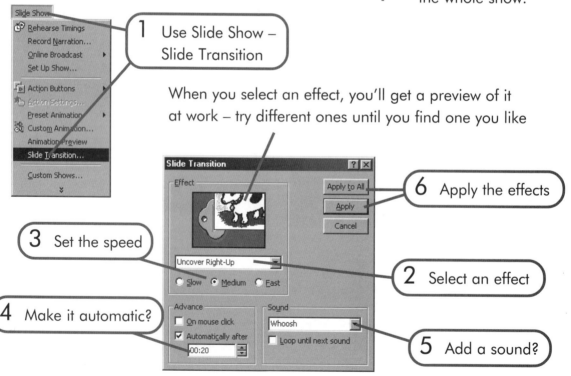

1 Use Slide Show – Slide Transition

When you select an effect, you'll get a preview of it at work – try different ones until you find one you like

6 Apply the effects

3 Set the speed

2 Select an effect

4 Make it automatic?

5 Add a sound?

100

Basic steps

Animation

1 Go to Slide Sorter view.

2 Open the Slide Show menu, point to Preset Animation and select a style.

3 View the show, or use Animation Preview to see how it looks.

This controls how the elements of a slide are brought into view. At the simplest, they are all in place when the slide is first displayed. At the most complex, you can specify a different animation for each element of every slide. In between, you can apply one animation style to the whole set – here's how.

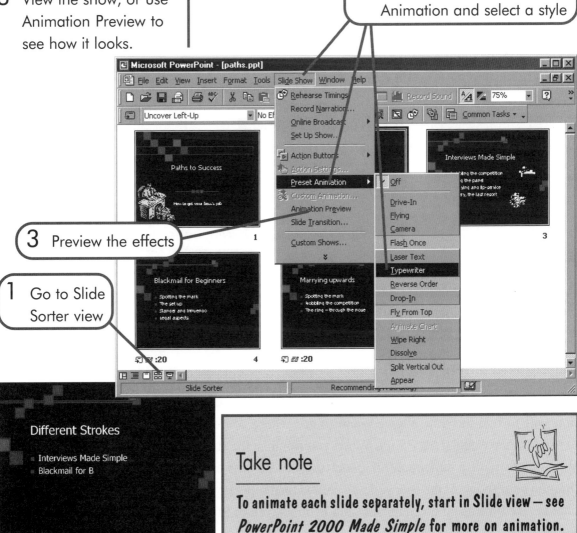

2 Use Slide Show – Preset Animation and select a style

3 Preview the effects

1 Go to Slide Sorter view

Take note

To animate each slide separately, start in Slide view — see *PowerPoint 2000 Made Simple* for more on animation.

Running a presentation

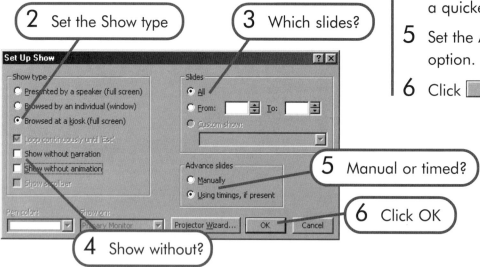

To run a slide show, you can simply click the Slide Show view button to start it, then click the left mouse button to bring up each slide. However, if you spend a few minutes beforehand you can ensure that it runs just how you want it, and if you make a little effort during the presentation, you can get more out of it.

The Setup

The main settings here are the Show type and the Advance slides. If you want a self-running demonstration, use the Browsed at a kiosk option, and timed advance.

2 Set the Show type

3 Which slides?

5 Manual or timed?

6 Click OK

4 Show without?

Rehearsing timings

Use the Rehearse Timings routine to check that your presentation will fit into the time allowed, and to see where you can expand or make cuts if necessary. When you run this, the slide show starts with a timer/control panel present as you talk through your show. At the end, you will see the total time; if you choose, the time spent on each slide can be displayed in Slide Sorter view.

Basic steps

1 Open the Slide Show menu and select Set Up Show…

2 Set the Show type.

3 For a partial show, set the From: and To: values.

4 Turn on the Show without … options for a quicker show.

5 Set the Advance slides option.

6 Click [OK].

Timings control panel

Time for current slide

Total time so far

Pause

Next

Redo last slide

Interactive presentations

The right-click menu that you can call up during a presentation, contains some useful tools.

The Pen Color should be selected in the Set Up Show dialog box to avoid delays during the show

● **Next**, **Previous**, the **Go** menu and **End Show** allow you to navigate freely through the show.

● The **Meeting Minder** lets you make notes and 'Action Items' as you go. These can all be called up from the **Tools** menu afterwards for reference, and – even better – the Action Items are automatically collated and displayed on a new slide at the end of the presentation.

● **Speaker Notes** displays any notes you added to a slide, in case you lose your way and your printed notes!

● **Screen** lets you black out the display temporarily.

● **Pointer Options** allow you to hide the pointer, or switch to a pen so that you can draw on the screen to emphasise a point.

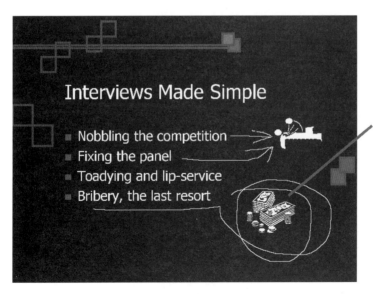

There's a real art to drawing smoothly on screen with a mouse – and very few of us ever acquire it!

Printing

As PowerPoint is based on slides, there is little room for variation in printing. The main choices are which parts of the presentation to print, which slides to include and how many copies. There is no Print Preview, such as in Word, as the output is the same on screen and paper, but there are two other previews.

● If the slides are for viewing by a browser, **Web Page Preview** will open your browser and display them.

● The Black and White view may be worth checking before output to a black-only printer. If you have images that do not come out well in the default black and white or grayscale, you can adjust their shading through the Black and White options on the image shortcut menu.

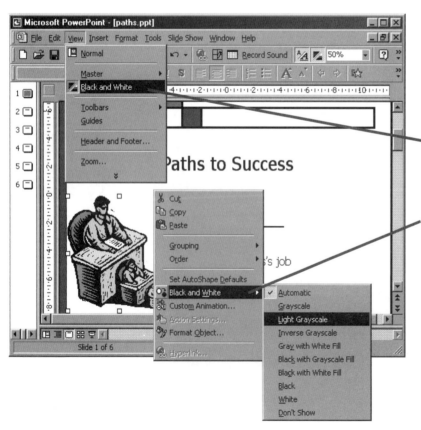

Use View – Black and White for the preview

If you need to adjust the shading of an image, right-click for the menu and select a Black and White option

Basic steps

❑ Instant print

1 Click 🖶.

❑ Controlled printing

2 Open the File menu and select Print.

3 Select a different Printer if required.

4 Set the range of pages or slides to print.

5 Set the number of copies.

6 Select a Print What option – *Slides*, *Handouts*, *Notes Pages* or *Outline view*.

7 For Handouts, set the number per page.

8 Set the other options as required.

9 Click [OK].

For a straight printout of all the slides (or to use the same settings as the last time you did a controlled print), just click the Print button. For anything else, use the menu command.

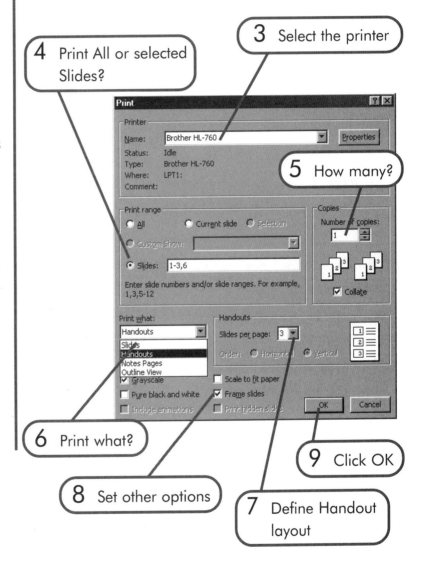

4 Print All or selected Slides?

3 Select the printer

5 How many?

6 Print what?

9 Click OK

8 Set other options

7 Define Handout layout

Summary

❑ A PowerPoint presentation can combine text with images, sound and video clips and objects from other applications.

❑ Use Blank Document to start a new presentation from scratch; a Design Template to start with a style colour and font scheme; AutoContent Wizard or the Presentation Templates for a ready-made structure.

❑ To enter text onto a slide, you must first create a text box.

❑ Pictures and other objects can be added through existing placeholders, or inserted at will.

❑ An Organization Chart can help to illustrate the personnel structure of an organisation.

❑ Use Slide Sorter view to rearrange the order of slides.

❑ You can set transitions to enliven the change from one slide to the next.

❑ There are animations that you can use to build a display one element at a time.

❑ Presentations can be set up to be run by a presenter or a viewer, or to be self-running.

❑ When printing in black and white, you can preview the output and adjust the shading of images if necessary.

❑ You can choose which part of the presentation and which slides to print.

7 Working with text

Selecting text

There are essentially two approaches to formatting text.

● You can set the style, type the text, then turn the style off, or set a new style.

● Or you can type in your text, then go back over it, selecting blocks and formatting them.

It is generally simplest to type the text first and format it to suit later – but before you can format it, you must select it.

These selection techniques apply to text in Excel cells and Powerpoint elements, and anywhere in Word documents.

Tip

You can select a word by double-clicking in it or a paragraph by triple-clicking in it.

Basic steps

❑ With a mouse

1 Point to the start of the text to be selected.

2 Hold down the left button, drag to the end and release the button.

❑ With the [Shift] key

3 Move the I-beam to the first character.

4 Hold down [Shift] and use the arrow keys to move to the end, then release [Shift].

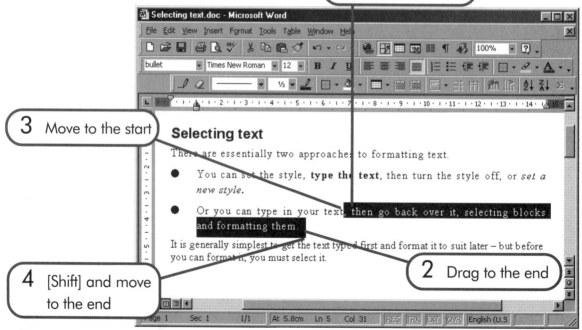

Select whole columns by
selecting their letters

Click here to select
the whole sheet

Select whole rows
by selecting their
numbers

You can select
and format a
block within a
cell

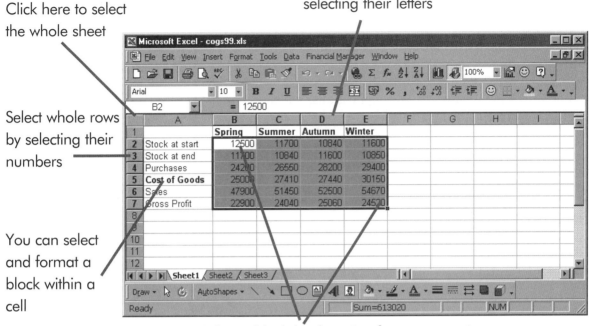

Select a block by dragging from
one corner to the opposite corner

To select one or
more elements,
drag an outline
to enclose them

Blocks within
the text can be
selected in the
usual ways

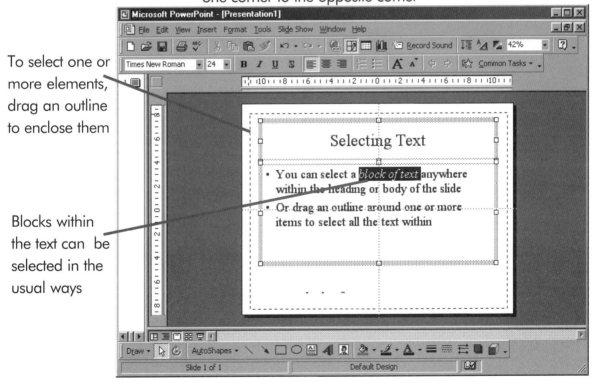

Fonts

The Formatting Toolbars

These hold all the tools you need for everyday work. There are minor differences between the applications, reflecting their different requirements.

Styles
(*page 58*)

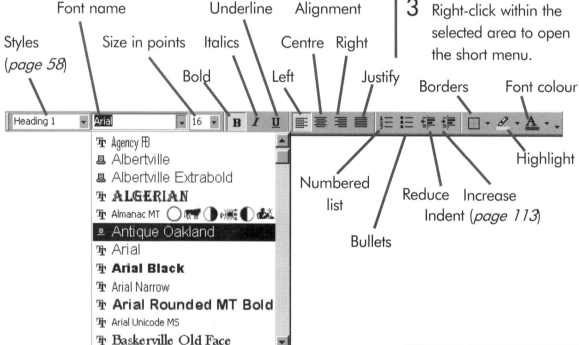

The Fonts dialog box

There will be times when the toolbars are not enough and you need to turn to the Fonts dialog box. Use this when you want to:

- set subscript, superscript, and other effects;
- convert headings to FULL or SMALL CAPITALS;
- check the suitability of a new font.

Basic steps

1 Select the text.

2 Click the Toolbar buttons to set fonts and styles.

or

3 Right-click within the selected area to open the short menu.

Tip

Some fonts are larger or heavier than others of the same size and style. Always choose your font before you change any of the other settings.

4 Select Font (Format cells in Excel).

5 Switch to the Font panel if it is not already open.

6 If you are going to change the font, *do this first.*

7 Set other effects as required, checking the appearance in the Preview pane.

8 Click [OK].

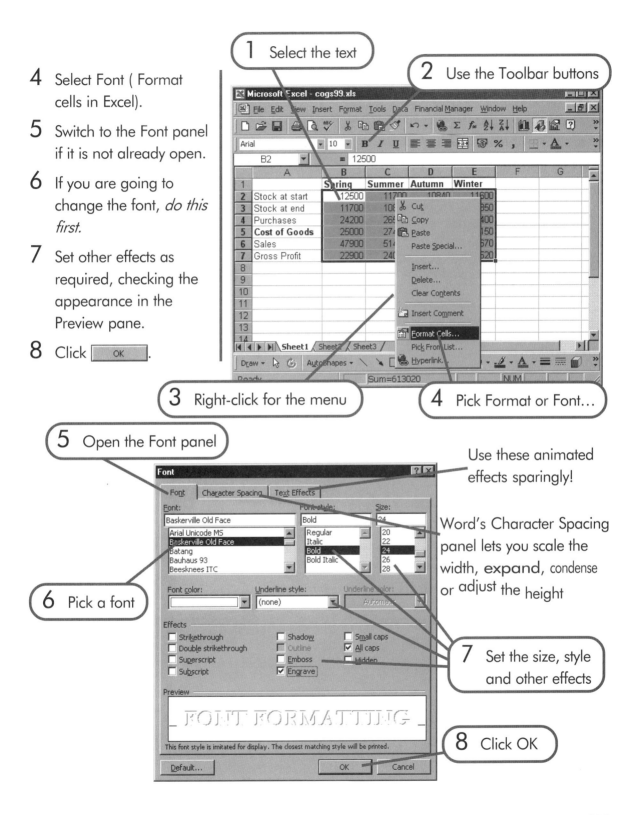

1 Select the text

2 Use the Toolbar buttons

3 Right-click for the menu

4 Pick Format or Font...

5 Open the Font panel

6 Pick a font

7 Set the size, style and other effects

8 Click OK

Use these animated effects sparingly!

Word's Character Spacing panel lets you scale the width, **expand**, condense or adjust the height

Alignment and Indents

Alignment

This refers to how text fits against the margins (or the edges of Excel cells). Four options are always available: Left, Right, Centre and Justify (aligned to both margins).

Excel also has other options to handle headings. You can:

- centre the text from one cell across a range of cells, perhaps to give a table a heading;

- set column labels vertical or at an angle.

Basic steps

- ❏ Centred headings

1 Select the cells that the text is to be centred in.

2 Click 🔛 – Centre Across Columns.

- ❏ Angled text

3 Select the cells

4 Right-click and select Format Cells...

5 Switch to Alignment.

6 Rotate the Text — pointer as desired

Text in A1 centred across A1 to E1

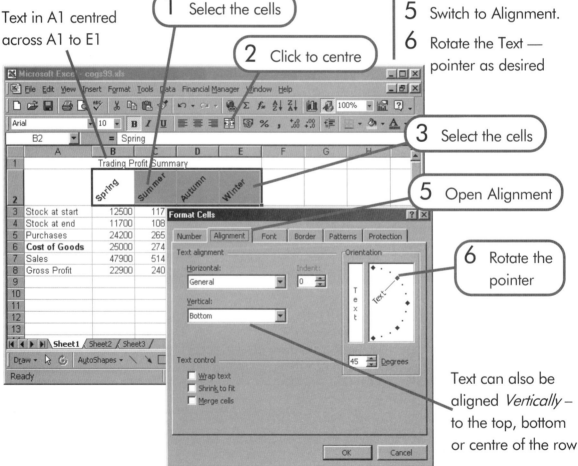

1 Select the cells

2 Click to centre

3 Select the cells

5 Open Alignment

6 Rotate the pointer

Text can also be aligned *Vertically* – to the top, bottom or centre of the row

Basic steps

1. Select the text.
2. Click ▣ (Word) or ➡ (PowerPoint) to indent.

or

3. Click ▣ (Word) or ⬅ (Powerpoint) to pull back out.

Indents

Indents set the distance from the edge of the page margins, or of the cells in Excel. In Word and PowerPoint, they can also be used to create a structure of headings and sub-headings.

Indenting is simplest with the buttons – each click pushes the text in (or out) 5mm.

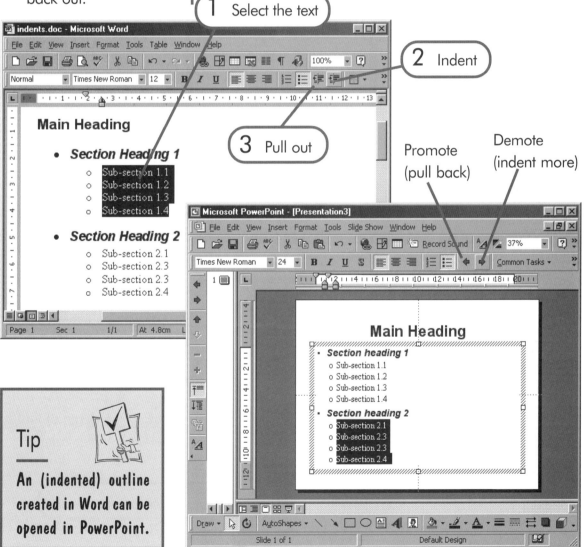

1 Select the text

2 Indent

3 Pull out

Promote (pull back)

Demote (indent more)

Bullets

In Word and PowerPoint, you can quickly add numbers or bullets to each item in a list by clicking ![icon] or ![icon]. For finer control, use **Format – Bullets and Numbering**.

These steps are for Word. Powerpoint is the same, except that you open the Symbol dialog box through the **Character** button.

Basic steps

1 Select the whole list.

2 Open the Format menu and select Bullets and Numbering.

3 Select the basic style.

4 Click Customize... .

5 Pick a bullet, or click Bullet... for more.

6 Select a font.

7 Hold the mouse button down for a close up – double-click to select.

8 Click OK .

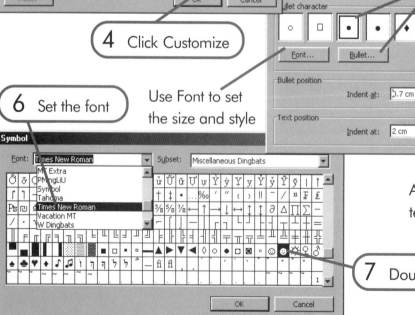

3 Set the basic style

4 Click Customize

5 Pick a bullet

Use Font to set the size and style

6 Set the font

Adjust the depth of the text and bullet indents

7 Double-click to select

Basic steps

- ❑ Simple numbering
1 Select the items.
2 Open the Format menu and select Bullets and Numbering.
3 Go to the Numbered tab and select a style.
4 Set the options as required.
- ❑ Outline Numbering
5 Start with the whole list, indented to set its structure.
6 Go to the Outline Numbered tab and select a style.
7 Click ▢ OK ▢.

Numbered lists

At the basic level, numbered lists are the same in Word and PowerPoint. However, they do have different options, reflecting their different natures – a (single) PowerPoint slide will rarely have more than two levels of numbering, but a Word document could have many levels of numbering, spread over many pages.

Word also has an **Outline Numbered** tab which sets different numbering styles for each level of indents.

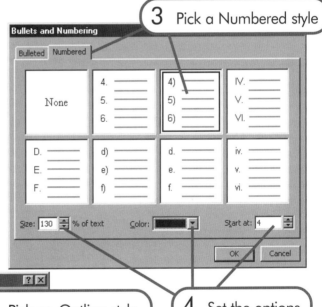

3 Pick a Numbered style

4 Set the options

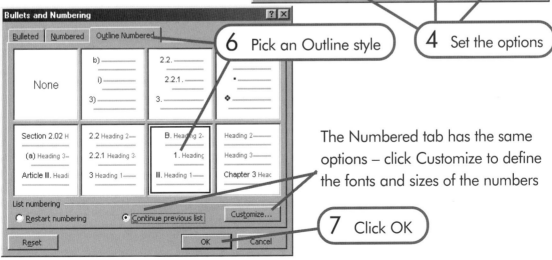

6 Pick an Outline style

The Numbered tab has the same options – click Customize to define the fonts and sizes of the numbers

7 Click OK

115

Autoformats

When word-processors added facilities for fancy fonts and layouts, productivity in many offices took a great leap *backwards*. Instead of simply typing and printing their documents, people spent time – often too much – prettying them up. Not enough people asked themselves if it was really worth the effort. The trouble is, if you want your documents to look 'professional', plain typing will no longer do. But don't worry, here's a great leap forward. The Autoformats in Word and Excel give you attractive documents *instantly*.

❑ Word Autoformat

1 Open the Format menu and select Autoformat.

2 Select Autoformat and review, then click OK.

3 When you get the Formatting completed message, click
    [Style Gallery...] .

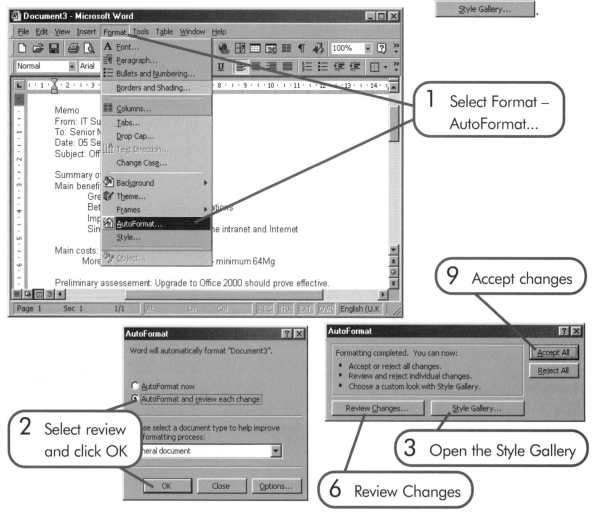

Basic steps

4 At the Style Gallery, select a style, checking it in the preview screen.

5 Click [OK] when you find one you like.

6 Click [Review Changes...].

7 Use the Find buttons to work through the changes and [Reject] any you don't like.

8 Click [Cancel] to end the review.

9 Click [Accept All].

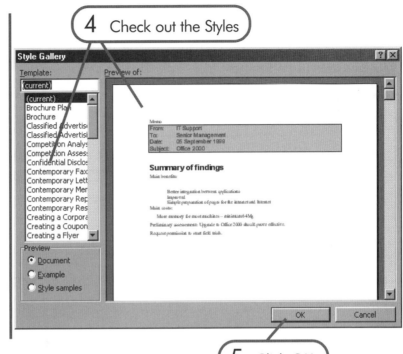

(4) Check out the Styles

(5) Click OK

The new format is shown here

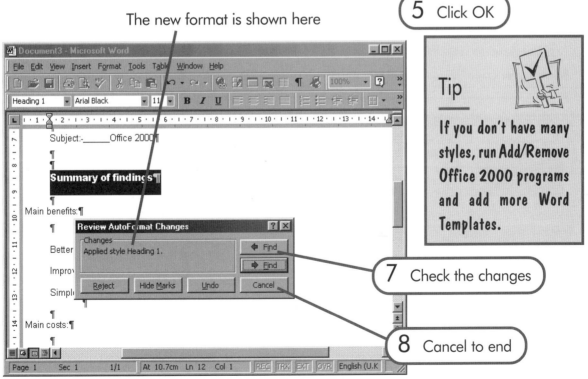

(7) Check the changes

(8) Cancel to end

Tip

If you don't have many styles, run Add/Remove Office 2000 programs and add more Word Templates.

AutoFormat Options

At some point, look at Word's **AutoFormat** options and set them to suit your preferences. If in doubt, leave options on. Later you can turn off those which do not prove to be useful.

Basic steps

1 At the Autoformat dialog box, click Options... .

2 Check those items that you want formatting.

3 Click OK .

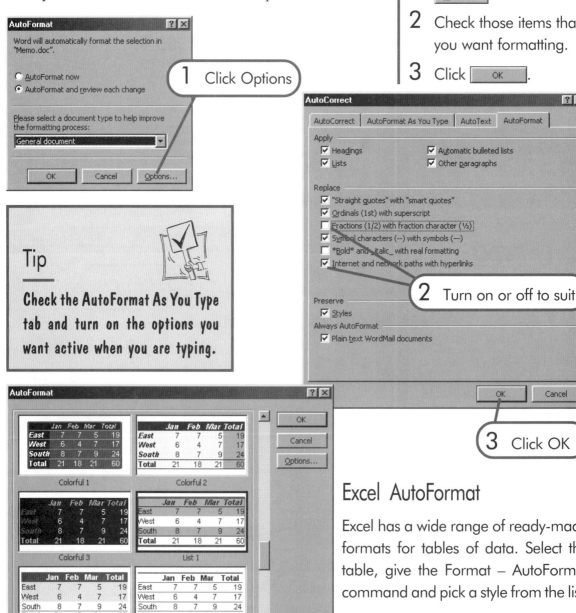

Tip

Check the AutoFormat As You Type tab and turn on the options you want active when you are typing.

Excel AutoFormat

Excel has a wide range of ready-made formats for tables of data. Select the table, give the Format – AutoFormat command and pick a style from the list.

Basic steps

❏ Word

1 At the AutoFormat dialog box, click `Options...` and go to AutoCorrect.

❏ Excel and PowerPoint

2 Open the Tools menu and select AutoCorrect.

3 Put a tick by those items you want corrected.

❏ Adding to the list

4 In the document, type the text correctly and select it.

5 Go to AutoCorrect.

6 Click Plain Text.

7 Enter the error or a character combination into the Replace slot.

8 Click `Add`.

Don't confuse this with the Spell Checker. Both correct typing, but AutoCorrect performs a one-for-one substitution from a limited list, rather than checking against a large dictionary. Use it to:

● correct common transpositions – **teh** into **the;**

● correct common misspellings – **acheive** into **achieve;**

● call up special characters – type **(c)** and AutoCorrect swaps it for ©.

You can add your own common 'typos' or substitutions to the list if they are not already there.

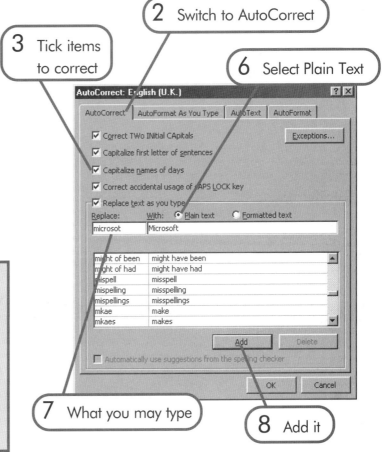

2 Switch to AutoCorrect

3 Tick items to correct

6 Select Plain Text

7 What you may type

8 Add it

Tip

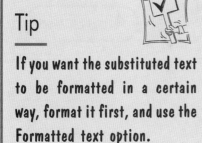

If you want the substituted text to be formatted in a certain way, format it first, and use the Formatted text option.

Exceptions for capitalising

AutoCorrect also checks that the first letters of sentences are capitals. As a sentence is defined as something that comes after a full stop, abbreviations can create problems. The solution is to have a list of abbreviations and not capitalise words that follow them. You can add to this list.

Are the other Capital rules right for you?

1 Open the AutoCorrect dialog box and click Exceptions...

2 Switch to the First Letter panel.

3 Type your new abbreviation in the Don't Capitalize After slot.

4 Click Add.

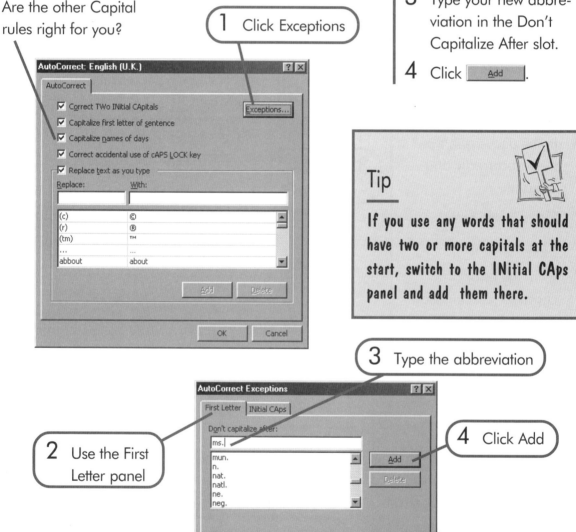

1 Click Exceptions

Tip

If you use any words that should have two or more capitals at the start, switch to the INitial CAps panel and add them there.

3 Type the abbreviation

2 Use the First Letter panel

4 Click Add

Basic steps

- ❑ Undoing one action
1 Click the arrow on the Undo button ↶▾.

- ❑ Undoing one action
2 Open the list from the Undo button ↶▾.

3 Point down the list to highlight all the actions that you want to undo.

4 Click the left mouse button.

Undo

In the old days, you were lucky if your software allowed you to undo a mistake. With the Office applications you can go back and undo a whole string of actions. This doesn't just protect you from the results of hasty decisions or self-willed mice, it gives you a freedom to experiment. You can do major editing or reformatting, and if at the end you preferred things how they were, you can undo your way back to it.

Redo

This is the undo-undo button! If you undid too much, use this to put it back again. Use it for the last action, or a whole sequence, exactly as with Undo.

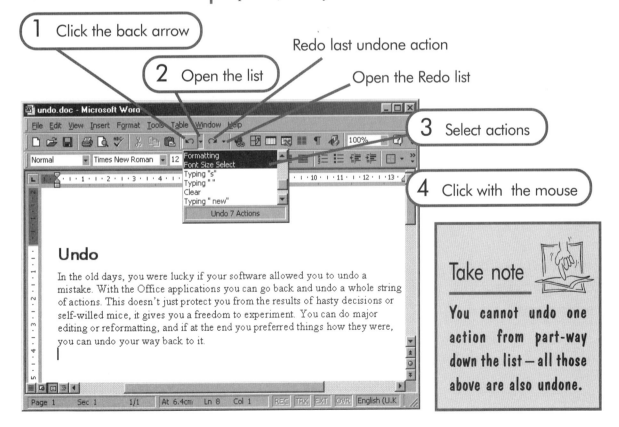

1 Click the back arrow

2 Open the list

Redo last undone action

Open the Redo list

3 Select actions

4 Click with the mouse

Take note

You cannot undo one action from part-way down the list – all those above are also undone.

Spelling

Spell checking is present in all Office applications. There is a good dictionary behind it, but it does not cover everything. Proper names, technical and esoteric words may be unrecognised and thrown up as 'errors'. These can be added to your own dictionary, so that they are not seen as errors in future.

Word and PowerPoint have a check-as-you-type option. You may prefer to just run a spell check after you have finished – especially if you have a lot to do and need to watch the keyboard rather than the screen!

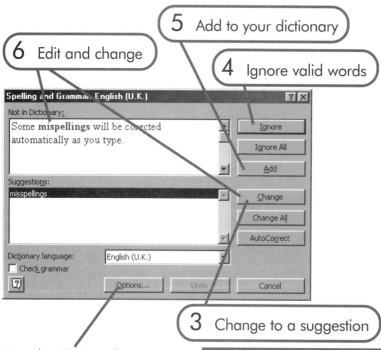

5 Add to your dictionary

6 Edit and change

4 Ignore valid words

3 Change to a suggestion

Use the Options button to set your preferences (see opposite)

Basic steps

1 If you want to check part of a document, or a block of cells in a spreadsheet, select it.

2 Open the Tools menu and select Spelling or click ☑.

❑ When a word is not recognised you can:

3 Select a Suggestion and click Change .

or

4 If it is a valid word click Ignore .

or

5 Add to put it in a custom dictionary.

or

6 Click in the Not in Dictionary slot, edit the word then click Change .

Take note

If you haven't already set up a dictionary for your own special words, click the Options button to open the Spelling options panel and use the Custom Dictionaries button.

Basic steps

1 On the Spelling dialog box, click Options.

2 Turn the settings on or off as desired.

❑ Fine-tuning grammar

3 Click Settings... .

4 Pick a Writing style.

5 Turn other checks on or off as desired.

6 Click OK .

Use this to find out how readable your text is. For an adult audience, aim for a readability of Grade 7 (a reading age of 12) – any lower is patronising; higher is hard work for most people.

Spelling and grammar options

Probably the key options here are whether or not to check spelling and grammar as you type – some people will find that it interrupts their flow, while others prefer to correct errors as they go.

Use this if you want to create specialist dictionaries for different types of jobs

2 Set options

Check as you type?

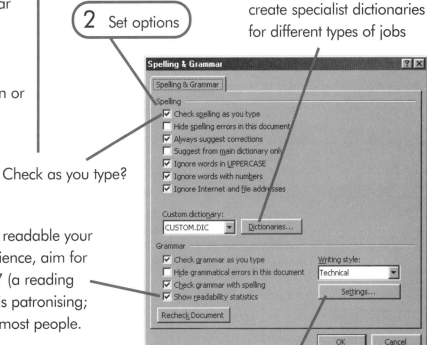

3 Click Settings

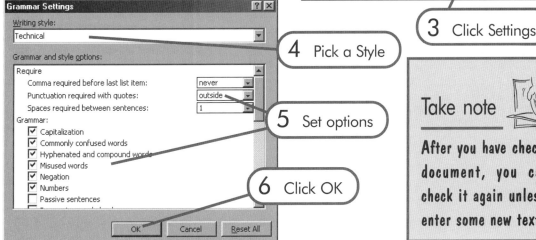

4 Pick a Style

5 Set options

6 Click OK

Take note

After you have checked a document, you cannot check it again unless you enter some new text.

Summary

❑ Text can be selected with either the mouse or keys, or a combination of both. Objects can be selected by clicking on them, or dragging an outline round them with the mouse. The same selection techniques apply in all applications.

❑ Font types, sizes and styles can be set from the Formatting toolbar or the Fonts dialog box. The dialog box also has additional control options.

❑ Text can be aligned to the Left or Right margins, Centred between them or Justified up to both.

❑ Indents give a structure to text.

❑ Bullets or numbers can be easily added to lists. The default bullets can be replaced by any characters you choose; numbers can be set in various styles.

❑ The Autoformat facility gives you standard formats for common documents and tables of data.

❑ The AutoCorrect routine recognises and corrects mistakes as you type. This may need customising to stop it 'correcting' intentional irregularities.

❑ If you make mistakes, you can Undo them – and if you undo too many actions, you can Redo them again!

❑ The Spelling checker has a good dictionary, and you can build your own to hold special terms and names that are not in the main one.

8 Other objects

Importing pictures

'A picture is worth a thousand words.' That philosophy can be applied to many types of documents.

- Your company logo will identify your letter and invoices;
- Products sell better if people can see pictures of them;
- Diagrams are often essential for communicating technical information and other complex concepts.

1 Open the Insert menu, point to Picture then select From File...

Or

2 Click  on the Picture toolbar.

3 Switch to the picture's folder.

4 If there are lots, use the Files of type box to filter out the right type.

5 Pick a picture, checking its preview.

6 Click `Insert`.

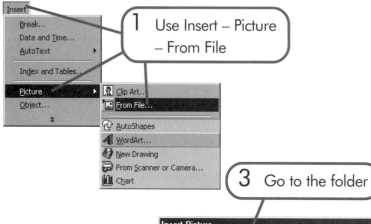

1 Use Insert – Picture – From File

3 Go to the folder

Tip

JPG, GIF, Photo CD and other graphics files can be imported if you have installed the graphic converters routines for them.

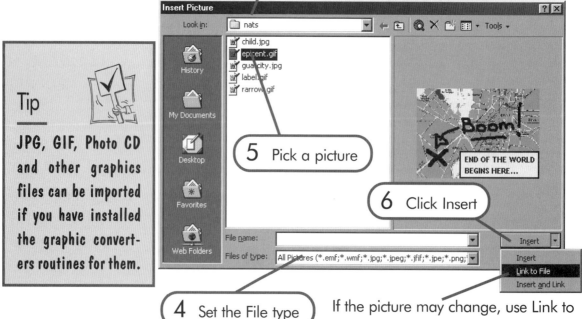

5 Pick a picture

6 Click Insert

4 Set the File type

If the picture may change, use Link to File to have it updated automatically

Basic steps

Clip art

1 Use Insert – Picture –
   Clip Art…

2 At the Pictures panel
   choose a Category.

Or

3 Type a Search word
   and press [Enter].

4 Click on a picture.

5 Click [⊞] to insert it;

   [🔍] to preview it;

   [⊞▸] to add it to your
   Favorites;

   [🔍▸] to find similar
   clips.

6 Close the Gallery.

Clip art pictures from the Clip Gallery can be inserted into any application – but don't overdo it. There's so much clip art around that you must use it selectively to have any impact.

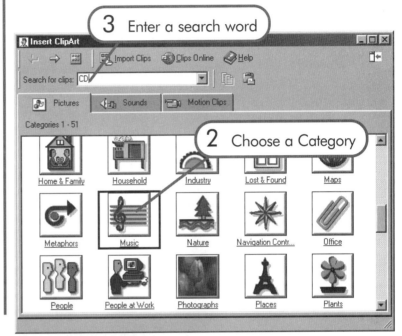

3 Enter a search word

2 Choose a Category

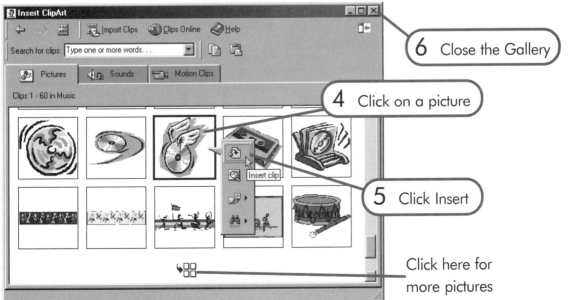

6 Close the Gallery

4 Click on a picture

5 Click Insert

Click here for
more pictures

Formatting pictures

The final appearance of any picture – clip art, file or drawing (see page 132) – can be adjusted at any point. Use the mouse to change the size, shape or position, or use the Picture toolbar or the Format Picture dialog box to add an outline, crop it, adjust the colours, or set how text wraps around it.

(see page 132)

Basic steps

1 Select the picture.

2 Drag a handle to adjust the size.

3 Drag anywhere within the area to move.

4 Use the Picture tools to adjust the settings.

Or

5 Right-click and select Format Picture, then work through the panels – you can adjust some settings more accurately here.

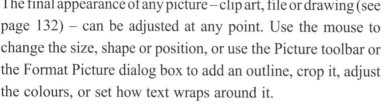

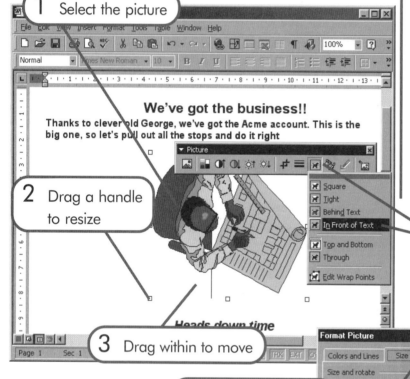

Use these for accurate size and position settings

Only drawn objects can be rotated

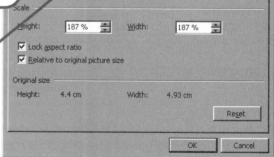

Take note

The options on some of the tools open the Format Picture dialog box at the relevant tab.

The Picture toolbar

Tip

You can get more clips from the Web — just click the Clips Online shortcut.

Insert new picture

More/less brightness

Line around image

Format picture

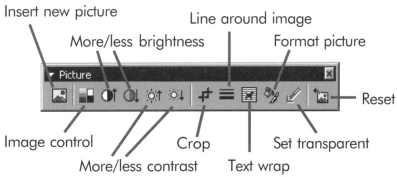

Reset

Image control

Crop

Set transparent

More/less contrast

Text wrap

Grayscale

Black & White

We've got the business!!

Thanks to clever old George, we've got the Acme account. This is the big one, so let's pull out all the stops and do it right

Heads down time

Grayscale and Watermark, used as background

Image control

The Image control menu gives you four options:

Automatic – in its normal colours;

Grayscale – for output to black-only printers, use with photographs and complex images;

Black & White – for high-contrast black-only printing, use with line-drawings or for special effects;

Watermark – ultra-pale, for use as background images.

Text wrap

This defines how the picture fits with nearby text – it can be surrounded by it, behind it, above it, or in a clear space of its own. Experiment with the options and see for yourself.

Set transparent

This can only be used on JPEG and GIF images. Select this and click on a colour, and that colour will become transparent so that the background colour shows through. It's much used on Web pages for round or other non-rectangular logos and images.

Sound and motion

As well as drawings and photographs, the Clip Gallery contains Sounds and Motion clips (animated GIFs). These can add a bit of sparkle to PowerPoint presentations or to Word or Excel documents that will be uploaded to the Internet/intranet, or sent to others via e-mail.

Sound are of two types: mid (MIDI) files play music; wav files are sound effects.

Basic steps

❑ Sounds

1 Open the Clip Gallery and go to Sounds.

2 Browse through the categories.

Or

3 Enter *sound* in the Search box.

4 Select a clip.

5 Click Play to test.

6 Click Insert.

7 In PowerPoint, you can set the sound to play when the slide appears or when you click on an icon.

8 In Word, the sound will be shown as an icon – double-click to play. Word only has Pause and Stop controls.

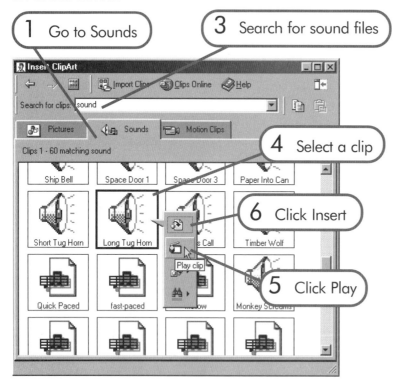

PowerPoint

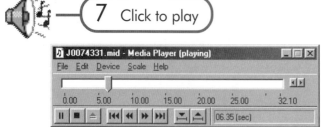

Word

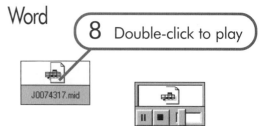

Basic steps

1 Open the Clip Gallery and go to Motion Clips.

2 Browse through the categories.

3 Select a clip.

4 Click Play to test.

5 Click Insert.

6 After the clip has been inserted, set its size and position as for an ordinary picture.

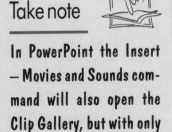

Take note

In PowerPoint the Insert – Movies and Sounds command will also open the Clip Gallery, but with only the Sounds and Motion Clips tabs available.

Motion clips

The previous version of Office had small selection of cartoon video clips. These have been replaced by a much larger selection of animated drawings and photographs. This was a good move – video clips take a lot of disk space and download time and rarely justify either. Motion clips files are typically around 10Kb.

The clips are all in animated GIF format, which can be displayed in any Web browser or Office application.

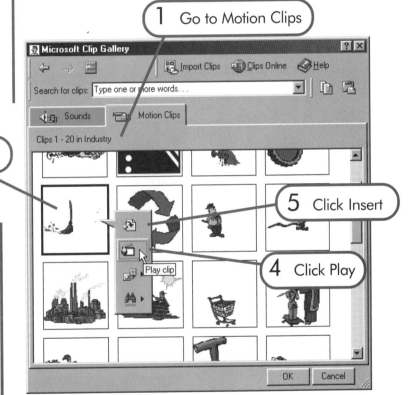

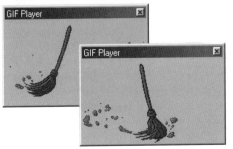

Most clips have their background set to 'transparent' so the slide or document colour shows through

Drawing pictures

If you want to create new diagrams or images, pick out points on imported pictures, or simply add arrows, blobs or blocks of background colour, there is a handy set of tools on the Drawing toolbar.

In a drawn picture, each item remains separate and can be moved, resized, recoloured or deleted at any later time. (Though items can be joined into Groups or placed inside picture frames, for convenient handling.) This is quite different from Paint and similar packages, where each addition becomes merged permanently into the whole picture.

The Draw menu lets you manipulate elements, singly or in groups

1 Click ▣ to open the Drawing toolbar.

2 Select an object tool and point and drag to create the item.

3 Adjust the fill and line colour and style.

4 To adjust an item, use the Selector tool and click on it. It can then be moved, resized, deleted or recoloured.

5 Double-click on an element to open its Format dialog box for fine-tuning its display.

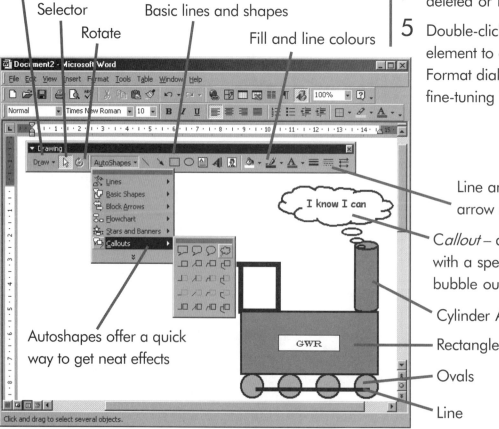

Selector

Rotate

Basic lines and shapes

Fill and line colours

Line and arrow styles

Callout – a text box with a speech/thought bubble outline

Cylinder Autoshape

Rectangle

Ovals

Line

Autoshapes offer a quick way to get neat effects

The drop-down palette has a set of basic colours, and access to the full palette (More Fill Colors...) and the Fill Effects dialog box

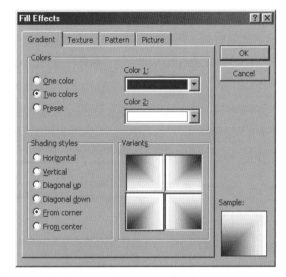

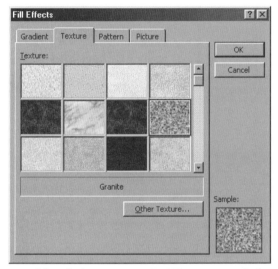

Fill Effects include Gradients and Textures – both good for the backgrounds of boxes. The same Patterns are available here as for Lines.

Double-click to open the Format... dialog box

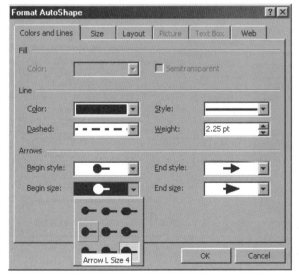

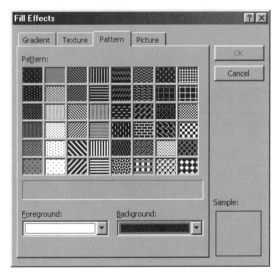

Patterned Lines are reached from the Line Colour panel. Try them for distinctive frames.

To add arrowheads, select from the Format dialog box.

Data maps

One of the clever little extras included in the Office 2000 package is Data Map – actually, not that little as it occupies over 6 Mb. This can take a table of geographical names and associated values – a *Sales by Country* summary, for example – and use it to create a map, with the relevant places shaded to show their relative importance. And it does it all by itself!

Basic steps

- ❑ Maps in Excel
- 1 Set up the data with names and values in adjacent, headed columns.
- 2 Select the data range.
- 3 Open the Insert menu and select Map... or select Object and pick Map from the list.
- 4 Drag an outline where the map is to go.

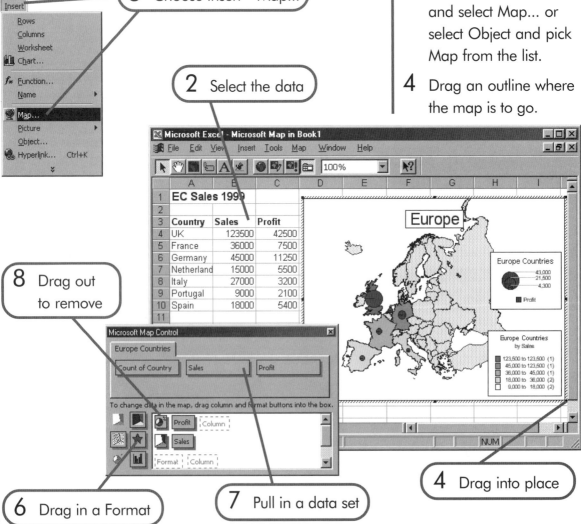

> **3** Choose Insert – Map...

> **2** Select the data

> **8** Drag out to remove

> **6** Drag in a Format

> **7** Pull in a data set

> **4** Drag into place

Potential problems

❑ Value indicators

If you have several sets of values or do not want to use shading...

6 Drag a Format button onto the Format label.

7 Drag a data set name onto the Column label.

8 Remove an unwanted column display by dragging its label or Format button out of the box.

Format styles

▨ Shading

▧ Block Colour

▦ Dot density

★ Graduated symbol

◓ Pie Chart

▮ Bar Chart

● The Data Map does have its limitations. It can handle the world, North and South America, US states, Europe and the UK, but not much else. You may see this panel:

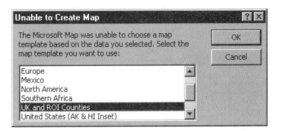

If you do select a map now, it will only be decorative, as the software will not be able to relate your names to any actual places.

● You may be given a choice of map. It doesn't matter if one covers too wide an area. You can set the display to zoom in on the relevant part.

● If the software cannot recognise a name, is will ask you for an alternative. For instance, it doesn't know about 'Holland' but will accept 'Netherlands'.

Annotating the map

There are three types of annotations available.

The Label tool will get the names and values from your data table.

The Pin tool will stick labelled pins in the map.

The Text tool can be used for any other text.

Basic steps

❑ Labels

1 Click �) .

2 At the Map Labels dialog box, select Names or Values.

3 With Values, if there are several sets, select the column.

4 Point at the area to be labelled and click. Repeat as needed.

5 Click elsewhere on the sheet to end.

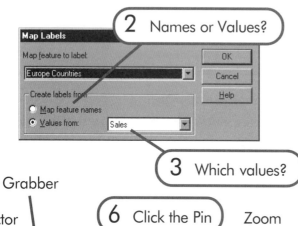

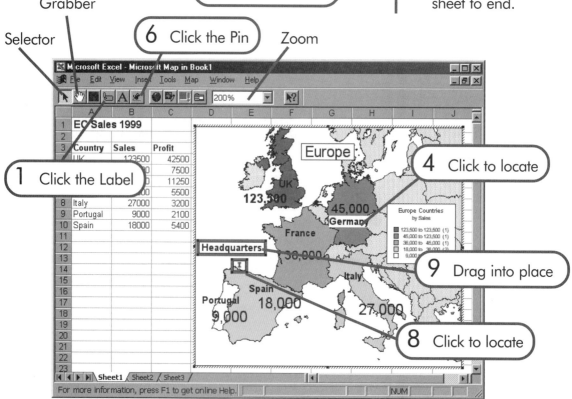

❏ Pins

6 Click .

7 At the Custom Pin Map dialog box, give a name for the file that will be created.

8 Click to place a pin, then type its label.

9 Click the Selector and drag the pin to move both, or the label to move it alone.

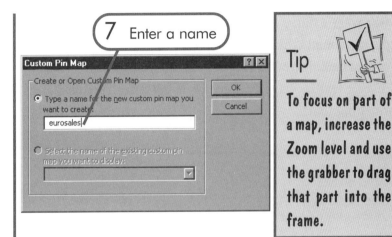

7 Enter a name

Tip

To focus on part of a map, increase the Zoom level and use the grabber to drag that part into the frame.

Basic steps

1 In Word or PowerPoint use Insert – Object and select Microsoft Map.

2 When the map appears select Insert – External Data.

3 Open the Access or Excel file, and select the data table.

4 Continue as for an Excel Data Map.

Maps in Word and PowerPoint

A Data Map can give impact to a report or presentation. Adding one is much the same as in Excel, with one key exception. When you insert a Map Object, you will get a standard (World) map. You must then link to an Access or Excel table to get the data.

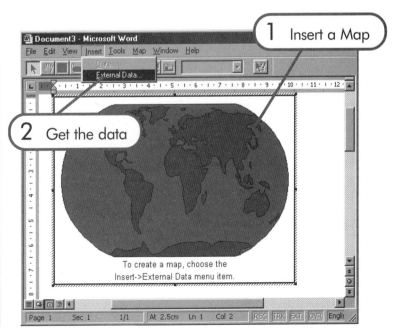

1 Insert a Map

2 Get the data

WordArt

If you want a fancy front cover for a report, or a high impact slide, you might like to investigate WordArt. It has some excellent facilities, but is very easy to use. With it, you can shape and style text in ways that go far beyond the standard Font Formatting tools.

Basic steps

1 Open the Insert menu and select Picture then WordArt.

2 Select a style from the Gallery.

3 Click OK .

4 Enter your text at the prompt.

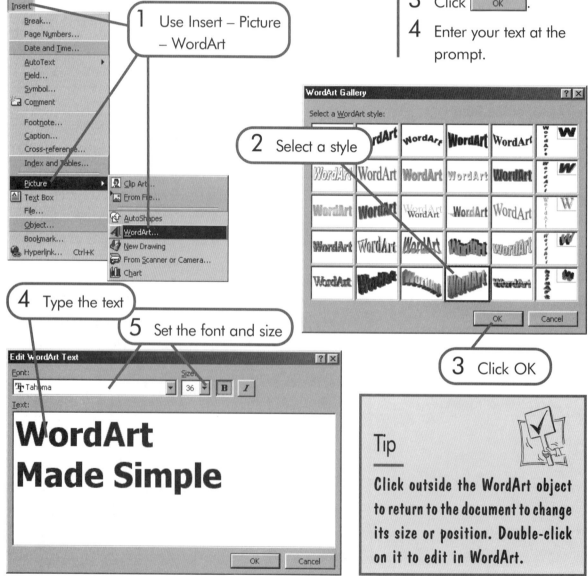

1 Use Insert – Picture – WordArt

2 Select a style

3 Click OK

4 Type the text

5 Set the font and size

Tip

Click outside the WordArt object to return to the document to change its size or position. Double-click on it to edit in WordArt.

5 Set the font and size.

6 Use the tools to adjust the shape, colour and other effects.

7 Click outside the WordArt area to end.

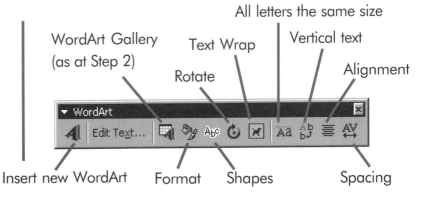

All letters the same size

WordArt Gallery (as at Step 2)

Text Wrap

Vertical text

Rotate

Alignment

Insert new WordArt   Format   Shapes   Spacing

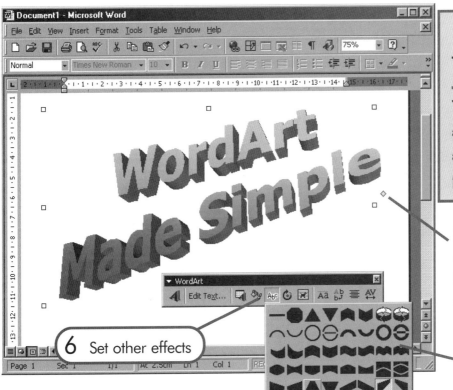

6 Set other effects

The Format options are almost the same as in Drawing – see page 133.

Drag the yellow diamond handles to adjust the curve or angle

The Shapes fix the outline of the text

Alignment options set the lines of text within the overall shape

Spacing options are mainly used where there are several lines of text

Tables

If you need to lay out data in neat columns and rows in Word or PowerPoint, the simplest way to do it is with a table. But tables can also be used for more than this.

You don't have to stick to a fixed grid – rows and columns can be varied in size, and cells can run across two or more cells or columns. This means that you can use a table as the framework for a display, ensuring that each element sits in the right place on the screen – this can be very useful when creating Web pages or non-standard PowerPoint slides.

In Word, there are additional Table tools that can be used to add sets of figures, or to sort rows or columns into ascending or descending order.

If you want to create a simple regular table, use the ▦ tool or the Insert – Table command. If necessary, rows and columns can be added or deleted later, or cells merged or split to produce more complex layouts.

If the table is to be used for layout, the ✐ tool will let you draw the outline and dividers where you want them.

❑ Simple tables

1 Place the cursor where the table is to go.

2 Click ▦ and drag the highlight across the grid to set the size.

Or

3 Use Insert – Table (in PowerPoint) or Table – Insert – Table (Word) and set the size and AutoFit option.

❑ Drawn tables

5 Use Table – Draw or click ✐ on the Tables and Borders toolbar.

6 Draw the table outline.

7 Draw lines across or down where needed – across the table or between existing lines.

8 Click ✐ again to turn the drawing mode off.

9 Enter the data into the cells, formatting the text as normal.

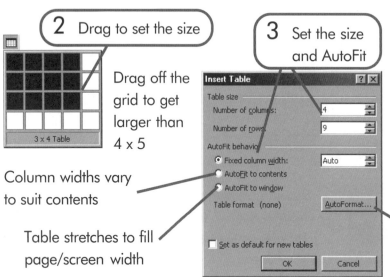

2 Drag to set the size

Drag off the grid to get larger than 4 x 5

3 x 4 Table

Column widths vary to suit contents

Table stretches to fill page/screen width

3 Set the size and AutoFit

Almost the same as Excel AutoFormats – see page 74

140

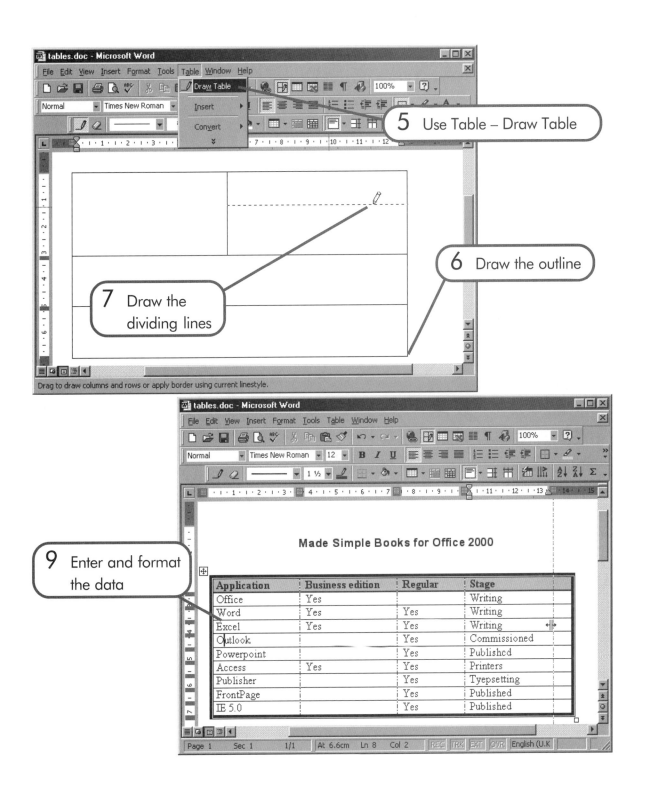

5 Use Table – Draw Table

6 Draw the outline

7 Draw the dividing lines

9 Enter and format the data

Made Simple Books for Office 2000

Application	Business edition	Regular	Stage
Office	Yes		Writing
Word	Yes	Yes	Writing
Excel	Yes	Yes	Writing
Outlook		Yes	Commissioned
Powerpoint		Yes	Published
Access	Yes	Yes	Printers
Publisher		Yes	Tyepsetting
FrontPage		Yes	Published
IE 5.0		Yes	Published

Modifying tables

A table's size, shape and layout can be changed at any time – even after data has been entered into it. You can:

- Insert or delete rows or columns;

- Split a cell into two or more rows or columns;

- Merge cells into one, across rows or columns.

In Word, the commands can all be found on the **Table** menu, with the most also present on the **Tables and Borders** toolbar.

PowerPoint has a more limited set of commands, and these can only be reached through its **Tables and Borders** toolbar.

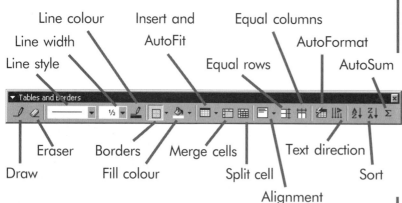

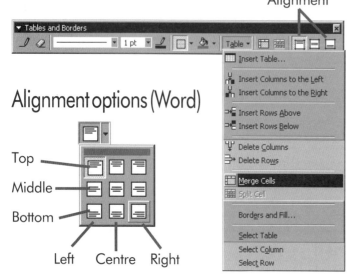

Alignment options (Word)

Top

Middle

Bottom

Left   Centre   Right

Basic steps

- ❏ Inserting rows/columns

1 Select a row/column adjacent to where the new one will go.

2 Select an Insert option from the Table menu.

- ❏ Deleting rows/columns

3 Select the rows/columns .

4 Select a Delete option from the Table menu.

- ❏ Merging cells

5 Select the cells and click 🔲.

Or

6 Select the Eraser 🖉 and rub out the line(s).

- ❏ Splitting cells

7 Select the cell and click ▦ then enter the new number of rows or columns.

Or

8 Select 🖊 and draw the line(s).

Basic steps

□ Borders

1 Select the cells.

2 Set the line style, width and colour.

3 Click the Border tool and select the lines to be styled.

Formatting tables

Text in cells can be formatted as normal. You can also:

● set the vertical and horizontal alignment of cell contents;

● format the the borders and the lines within the table – this is slightly tricky (see the Steps);

● change the background colour of selected cells.

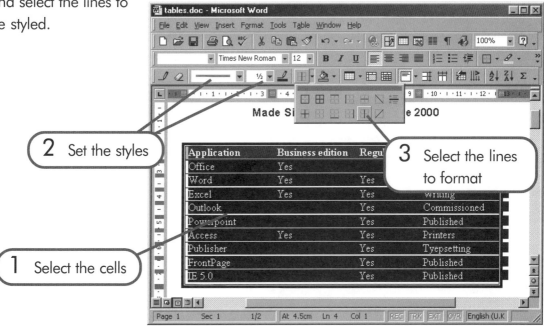

2 Set the styles

3 Select the lines to format

1 Select the cells

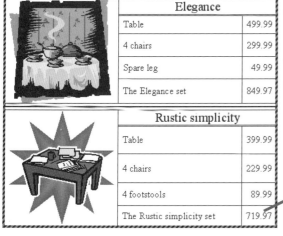

Elegance	
Table	499.99
4 chairs	299.99
Spare leg	49.99
The Elegance set	849.97

Rustic simplicity	
Table	399.99
4 chairs	229.99
4 footstools	89.99
The Rustic simplicity set	719.97

Table used mainly for layout – this was drawn, but could have been started as a 10 × 3 grid, with cells merged across rows on the left, and across columns for the two titles.

Total found by selecting this cell and clicking AutoSum to add the column of figures above it (it can also add a row to its left)

Quick graphs

If you want to knock up a quick chart or graph in a Word or PowerPoint document, the Graph 2000 software will do the job. It gives you a datasheet and related graph, set up with dummy data. All you have to do is replace that data with your own. If you care to spend the time, you can also change the chart style, colours and other aspects of its appearance.

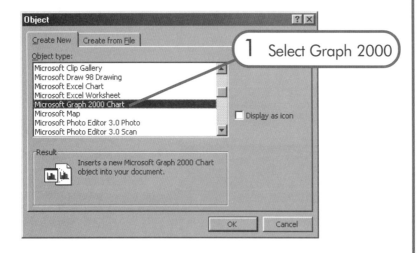

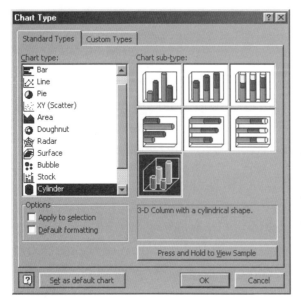

Basic steps

1 Open the Insert menu, select Object then Graph 2000.

2 Type your data into the datasheet, adding more columns or rows if needed.

3 Use the tools to change the display – most toggle features on and off.

4 Select an item from the chart and right-click for its formatting options.

Or

5 Select the element from the drop-down list and click the Formatting button.

6 Click back into the document and adjust the graph's size.

The default chart is an upright bar style, but you have plenty of choice! There is a full range of normal chart types on the Standard tab – and some striking ones on the Custom tab.

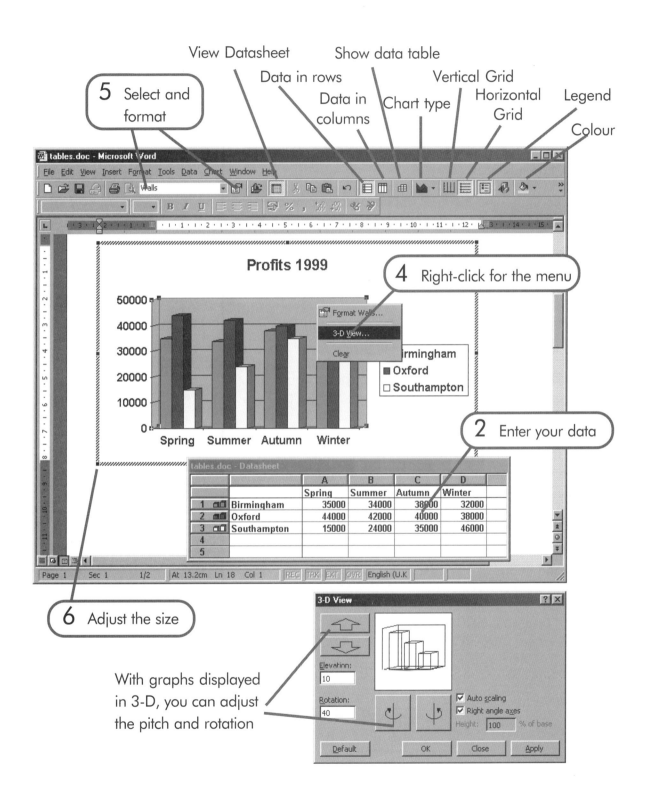

View Datasheet

Data in rows

Show data table

Data in columns

Vertical Grid

Chart type

Horizontal Grid

Legend

Colour

5 Select and format

tables.doc - Microsoft Word

File Edit View Insert Format Tools Data Chart Window Help

Walls

Profits 1999

4 Right-click for the menu

Format Walls...

3-D View...

Clear

Birmingham

■ Oxford

□ Southampton

50000

40000

30000

20000

10000

0

Spring   Summer   Autumn   Winter

2 Enter your data

tables.doc - Datasheet

			A	B	C	D	
			Spring	Summer	Autumn	Winter	
1		Birmingham	35000	34000	38000	32000	
2		Oxford	44000	42000	40000	38000	
3		Southampton	15000	24000	35000	46000	
4							
5							

Page 1   Sec 1   1/2   At 13.2cm Ln 18   Col 1   REC TRK EXT OVR   English (U.K

6 Adjust the size

With graphs displayed in 3-D, you can adjust the pitch and rotation

3-D View

Elevation:
10

Rotation:
40

☑ Auto scaling
☑ Right angle axes
Height: 100   % of base

Default   OK   Close   Apply

145

Summary

❏ You can import clip art, pictures and other images in most common graphics formats into any Office application, to illustrate or enhance a document.

❏ There is a huge and varied set of Clip Art pictures in the Clip Gallery.

❏ You can fine-tune the final appearance of any inserted picture through the Formatting options.

❏ Sound and Motion clips can be inserted into any documents – though they are probably best reserved for PowerPoint presentations.

❏ The Drawing tools can be used to creat diagrams or add lines, arrows or other simple graphics.

❏ The Data Map will convert a table of geographic names and related data into a map, with shading to show the relative values.

❏ WordArt can be used for headings, splashes and background text. It gives you far more varied effects than the normal formatting tools.

❏ Tables can be used to hold text in regular rows or columns, and also to set the framework for positioning text and images.

❏ To produce a graph from a small table of data quickly, insert a Graph 2000 object.

9 Sharing data

Alternative approaches

There are a number of different ways to share data between applications. The first three bring a selected object or block of data into a second application. They use the Edit Copy and Paste commands in various ways.

- **Simple paste** – the text, table, picture or whatever becomes an integral part of the host document, dropping all connection to the application in which it was created. Use this method where the host document's application can handle any editing or reformatting that you might want to do to the pasted-in data.

- **Embedding** – the pasted-in data forms an independent object within the document. It loses its connection to the original data, but can be edited by its own application *within the host document*. Use this method if you want to be able to edit the object using its original application.

- **Linking** – the pasted-in data retains a full connection to the original data and its application. Any changes in the source data are automatically reflected in the copy, and the original file can be edited – by calling up its application – from within the host document. This is the method to use for reports and presentations where you want to ensure that all the data is up to date.

The Copy and Paste commands work by means of the Clipboard, an area of memory separate from any application. Data stored in the Clipboard from within one application can then be accessed from within any other. If necessary it can be converted into a new format for the target application. There are a few situations where Copy and Paste will not work between applications because of fundamental differences in formats, but there is never a problem in copying data between any Office applications.

Take note

Most of the methods described here use OLE – Object Linking and Embedding. This is a standard Windows facility that can be used for sharing data between any Windows applications, not just the Office 2000 set.

Tip

The Clipboard in Office 2000 has been greatly improved – see page 158.

Copy and Paste

The first step in sharing data is to go to the source document, select the object or block of text and copy it, using either the **Edit – Copy** command or . What you do then depends upon whether you want to copy, embed or link the data, and what format you want it in.

- Use or **Edit – Paste** to copy in the data. It will come in as Formatted Text or Picture, as applicable.

- Use **Edit – Paste Special** to embed or link, or to select your own format for copied data.

Paste As formats

- **Word, Excel, PowerPoint** (or other) **Object** – use this for embedding;

- **Formatted Text** – the text retains its fonts, styles, etc., but may be edited by the host application;

- **Unformatted Text** – plain text, editable by the host;

- **Picture** and **Bitmap** – scalable graphics; pictures can give better printed images.

- **HTML** – formatting simplified, retaining only features supported by HTML. Use when creating Web pages.

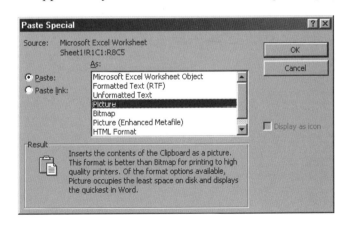

Copying

Using the and 🖹 buttons is the quickest and simplest way to get data from one application into another, but the data is pasted differently in different applications.

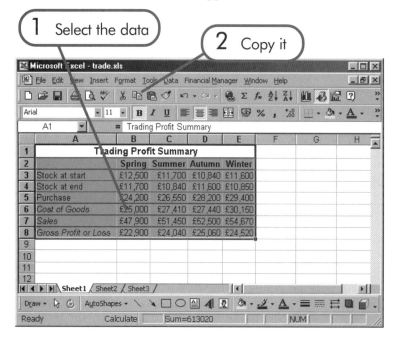

(1 Select the data)

(2 Copy it)

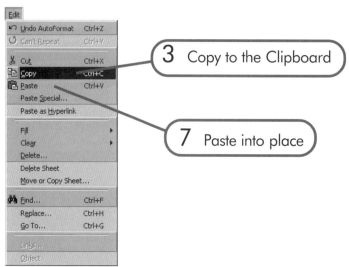

(3 Copy to the Clipboard)

(7 Paste into place)

Basic steps

1 In the source application, select the object or block of text or cells to be copied.

2 Click 🖻.

or

3 Pull down the Edit menu and select Copy.

4 Go to the host document.

5 To paste as *text*, point the cursor to where the data is to be placed.

6 Click 🖺.

or

7 Pull down the Edit menu and select Paste.

Tip

If you do a lot of copy and paste work, learn the keyboard shortcuts:

[Ctrl] – [C] to copy

[Ctrl] – [V] to paste

Excel to Word

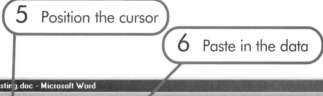 or **Edit – Paste** brings in the data in Rich Text Format, and creates a Word table.

● As it is *text*, it can be edited within Word in the usual fashion;

● As it is *Rich Text*, its font, size, borders, etc. are retained.

5 Position the cursor

6 Paste in the data

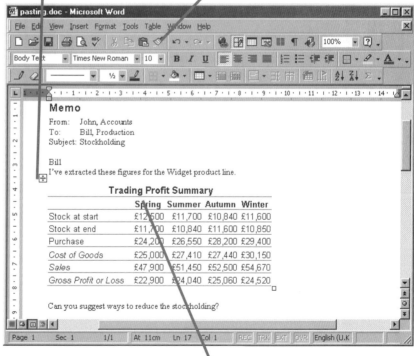

Individual columns and rows, and the contents of any of the cells can be edited and reformatted as needed.

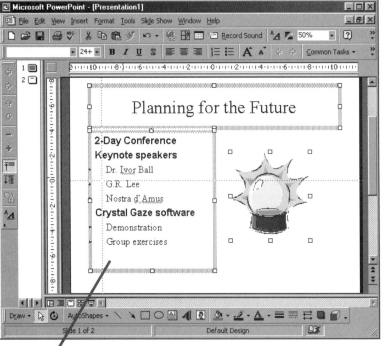

Selected objects can be pasted in as a single picture.
This can be scaled or cropped to size.

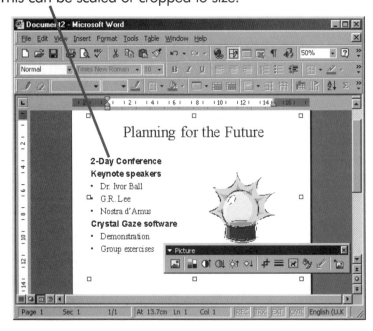

❑ If you select a group of objects from a slide, then Paste them, the objects come in separately, and the text and pictures can be edited within Word. However, PowerPoint uses BIG font sizes, and the pasted objects are likely to swamp your document.

❑ If the objects are going to illustrate a Word document, use Paste Special, and bring them in as a Picture for a easier handling.

❑ If you want to take text from PowerPoint into Word, use Paste Special and bring it in as unformatted text – it will be far smaller!

Word to PowerPoint

- ❏ However you paste, all formatting is retained, though font sizes are normally increased.

- ❏ If you 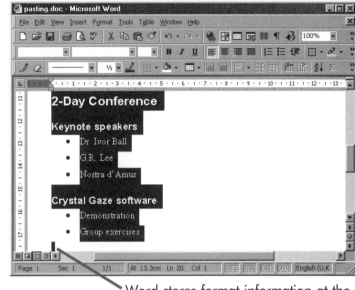 Word text onto a blank area, each paragraph becomes a text box.

- ❏ If you Paste into a *Click to add text* area of a bullet list, the text will have (extra) bullets added.

Word stores format information at the end of paragraphs – copy an extra line to make sure all the text is formatted.

A simple Paste brings Word text in as a set of text boxes

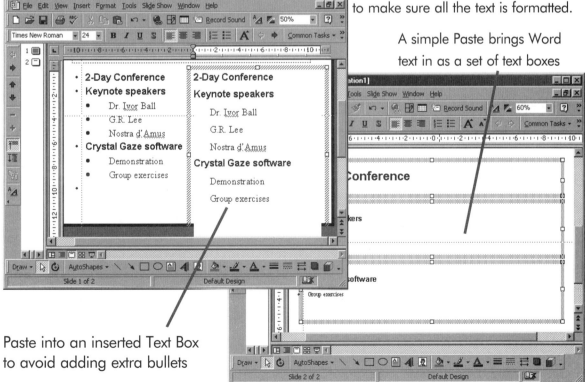

Paste into an inserted Text Box to avoid adding extra bullets

Embedding

Sometimes a simple Paste embeds an object – e.g. an Excel table in a PowerPoint slide – but to be certain that an object is embedded, it is best use the Paste Special command.

4 Select Paste

3 Use the Object format

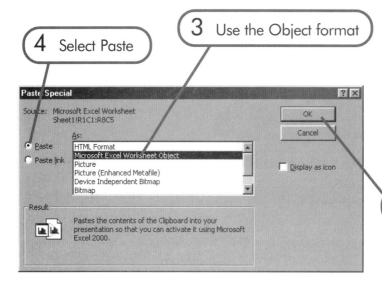

5 Click OK

1 Select the object to be pasted.

2 In the target document, use Edit – Paste Special…

3 Set the As option to an Object of the original application.

4 Select Paste.

5 Click [OK].

When you edit an embedded object, the menus and toolbars change to suit the object.

Take note

The embedded object is only a copy of the original data. If you edit an embedded object, it does not affect the data in the original file and vice versa.

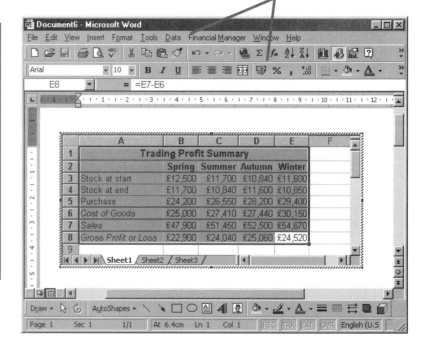

Basic steps

❑ Edit within the host

1 Double-click on the object to open a limited version.

Or

2 Right-click to open the short menu and choose Object – Edit.

3 Edit and click anywhere off the object to close the application.

❑ Edit in the application

4 Right-click to open the short menu and choose Object – Open.

5 Edit, and use Close and Return... to exit.

Editing embedded objects

Working simply within the host application, you can change the size and position of an embedded object. If you want to edit or reformat its contents, you must use its original application. You can do this at two levels:

● run a limited version, within the host application;

   or

● open the full version of the original application and work on the object there.

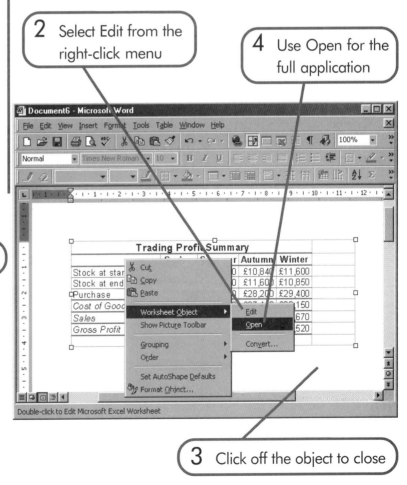

2 Select Edit from the right-click menu

4 Use Open for the full application

5 Use Close and Return

3 Click off the object to close

155

Linking

The one crucial difference between embedding and linking is that with a linked object, there is only one set of data. When you edit the original file – the source data – the contents of the linked object are changed to match.

1 Copy the block of text or object to be linked.

2 In the host document, open the Edit menu and select Paste Special.

3 Select Paste Link.

4 If you have a choice of As formats, select the most suitable one for the job.

5 Click OK.

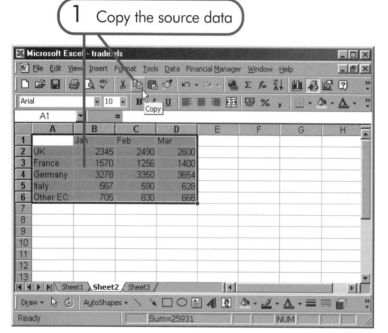

1 Copy the source data

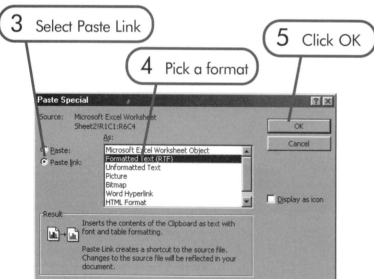

3 Select Paste Link

4 Pick a format

5 Click OK

Tip

The type of data that is being linked in determines the choice of As formats. When in doubt, use the Object format.

Editing linked objects

All linked objects can be edited by double-clicking on them to call up their original application. Those pasted in the Object format can only be edited this way.

In Object, Picture or Bitmap format, you can alter the size and position of the linked object.

With Formatted or Plain Text, you can also edit them using the host application's tools – though these edits will only last until the link is updated. This is only worth doing if you want to prettify something for immediate printing.

The month names have been edited to appear in full in this linked object. (Compare them with the Excel table opposite.) However, as soon as that Excel file is edited, or when the file is next opened, the link will be updated and the original headings restored.

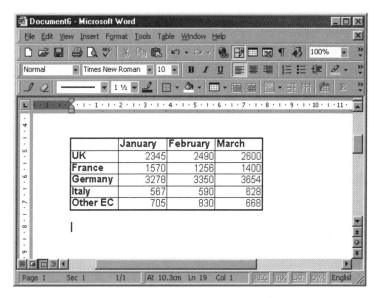

	January	February	March
UK	2345	2490	2600
France	1570	1256	1400
Germany	3278	3350	3654
Italy	567	590	628
Other EC	705	830	668

The Office Clipboard

If you are used to Windows, you will know that when you copy data into the Clipboard, the new data replaces whatever was there previously. This is no longer true with Office 2000, where the Clipboard can hold up to 12 items. As these can be pasted individually or all at once, it can be very useful for reorganising documents and for collating data from a variety of sources.

There are two limitations that you should note:

- When you do a **Paste All**, the items are pasted in the order in which they were copied.

- Individual items cannot be deleted from or moved within the Clipboard.

Basic steps

❑ Reorganising data

1 If the Clipboard is not visible, right-click on a toolbar and select Clipboard.

2 Move within or between applications, copying items in the order that you want them to appear.

3 Move to where you want to paste and click Paste All .

4 To empty the Clipboard, click .

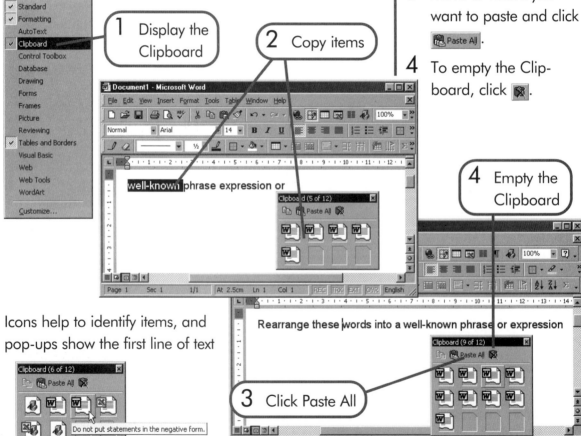

Icons help to identify items, and pop-ups show the first line of text

Inserted objects

Complete files can be linked into documents using the **Insert Object** command. Though the whole file is linked, not all of it will be displayed – you will see part of a Word or Excel document, or the first slide of a presentation. If you edit it, you can access the rest, or scroll to a different part of the document to change the visible area.

Inserted file objects can be:

- created at the time, from within the host document, or loaded in from file;

- either embedded or linked;

- displayed normally or present just as icons. In either case, the Edit and Open options for the source application are on the short menu.

The menus that you get when you right-click on an object depend mainly on the application, though the Object sub-menus vary with the nature of the object.

Word object (in Excel)

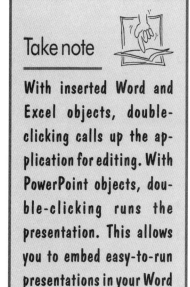

Excel object (in PowerPoint)

PowerPoint object (in Word)

With a linked object, Edit and Open both call up the full application. If the object is not linked, Edit gives you the limited version of the application, within the host document.

Inserting an object

Once you have decided what you want to insert, and whether to place it as an icon or displayed object, the actual insertion is easy.

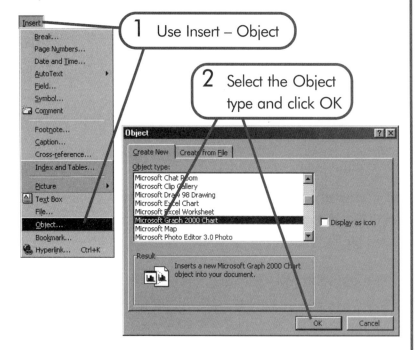

1 Use Insert – Object

2 Select the Object type and click OK

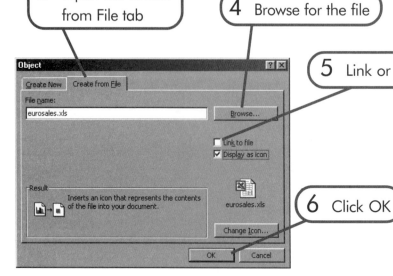

3 Open the Create from File tab

4 Browse for the file

5 Link or embed?

6 Click OK

Basic steps

1 Open the Insert menu and select Object.

❏ Creating a new file

2 On the Create New tab, select the Object type and click OK. The application will open within the document.

❏ Using an existing file

3 Open the Create from File tab.

4 Click [Browse...] to locate the file.

5 Turn on Link to file, if wanted, or leave it off to embed the file.

6 If you want the file as a visible object, click [OK].

Take note

Create from File is an option, not a tab, in PowerPoint.

1 Follow steps opposite to to select the Object type or file.

2 Turn on the Display as Icon option.

3 Click [Change Icon...].

4 Check out icons in the list to see if there is one you prefer.

5 Replace the filename with a brief Caption.

6 Click [OK].

If you want your readers to open (or run) the linked file to see it properly, it may be better to place it as an icon. Most computer users nowadays need little prompting to click an icon, though they may well need prompting to click on a spreadsheet table, block of text or other image.

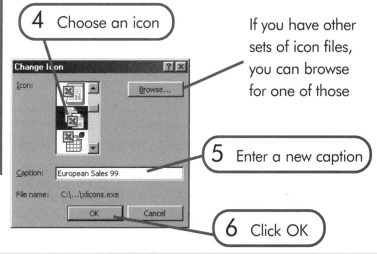

4 Choose an icon

If you have other sets of icon files, you can browse for one of those

5 Enter a new caption

6 Click OK

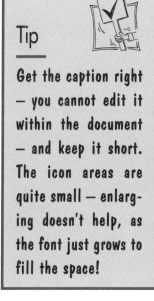

Tip

Get the caption right — you cannot edit it within the document — and keep it short. The icon areas are quite small — enlarging doesn't help, as the font just grows to fill the space!

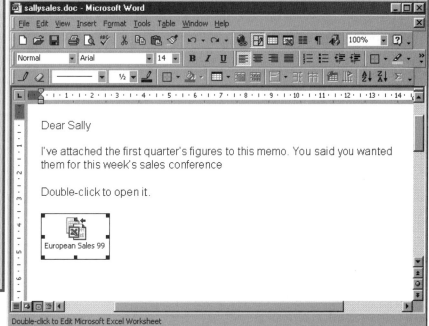

Dear Sally

I've attached the first quarter's figures to this memo. You said you wanted them for this week's sales conference

Double-click to open it.

European Sales 99

Summary

❑ The Edit – Copy and Paste commands can be used to copy data from one application to another. Depending upon the type of data and the applications, the copy may become an integral part of the target document, or may be embedded in it.

❑ Embedded objects can be edited by calling up their original application from within their new document.

❑ Linked objects retain the connection to their original file. If this is edited, the changes will be seen in the new document.

❑ Data can be pasted or paste linked into a document, in a variety of formats. The choice of formats depends upon the type of data and the source application.

❑ The Office Clipboard can hold up to 12 separate blocks of copied data. They can be pasted individually or all at once – in their stored order.

❑ Files from different applications can be included in documents as Inserted objects.

❑ Linked and Inserted objects can be displayed in their normal format or as icons.

10 Binders

Binders and sections

The concept of the Binder is simple but effective. If you have a number of documents – from the same or different Office applications – that are regularly used together, you can store them in one binder file, rather than in separate application files.

Working in the Binder, you can:

- keep related files together, opening and saving all the documents in one operation;

- print all of the documents at once – though selected documents can also be printed individually;

- quickly and easily switch from one application to another and copy formats, styles and data between them.

Sections

The documents in a binder file are referred to as *sections*. Once it has been set up, you would normally leave the composition of a binder alone, but it is not fixed permanently. An existing file can be inserted into a binder as a new section, and sections, created within a binder, can be saved as separate files.

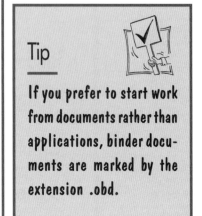

Tip

If you prefer to start work from documents rather than applications, binder documents are marked by the extension .obd.

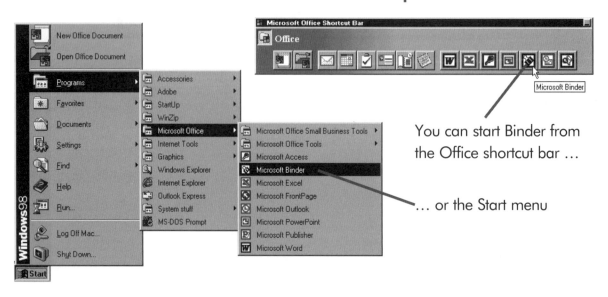

You can start Binder from the Office shortcut bar ...

... or the Start menu

164

The Binder display

The Binder itself is little more than a means of holding and accessing documents. It offers an almost blank display and a limited menu. Once you have opened a binder file, the display will be dominated by the application of the current document within the binder.

The slim panel down the left side is the means of navigating between documents. It can be tucked out of the way when not needed, by clicking ⊞ on the far left of the menu bar.

Click here to open and close the navigation bar down the left-hand side

The Section menu is added to every 'bound' application's menu bar

Double click to switch to the document

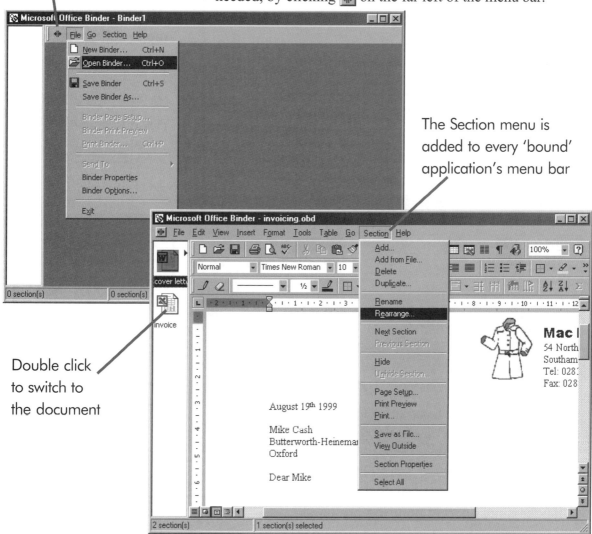

Creating a new binder

New binders can be created from scratch, either from the blank start-up screen or with a Blank Binder.

If you regularly produce sets of documents to the same patterns – e.g. for each client or project – then the outline documents can be saved as a template, to provide a fast start next time.

❑ Creating from scratch

1 Run Binder – that's it, you're ready to start a new binder.

Or

2 If Binder is already running (with an existing file), open the File menu and select New.

3 Select Blank Binder.

❑ Using a template

4 Pick a template.

5 Click ▭OK▭.

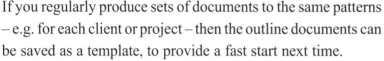

2 Use File – New Binder

3 Select Blank Binder

4 Select a template

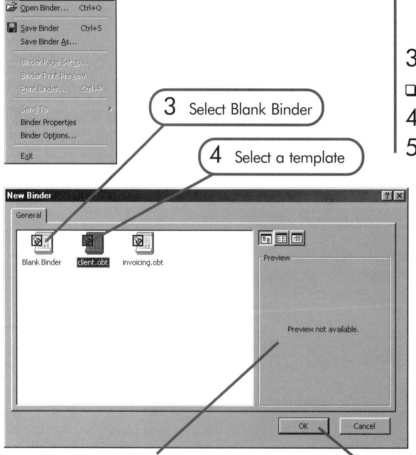

Tip

You can also start a new binder from the New Office Document window – select Blank Binder or a template.

The Preview will sometimes show the layout and style of the first document – Binder is not good at handling previews!

5 Click OK

Basic steps

Adding sections

❑ To create a document

1 From the Section menu select Add.

2 Open a panel and select a template.

3 Click OK.

❑ To add from file

4 From the Section menu select Add from File.

5 At the Add from File dialog box, pick a file.

6 Click 🗁 Add .

The documents that are bound into it can be created from new – within the binder – or pulled in from existing files.

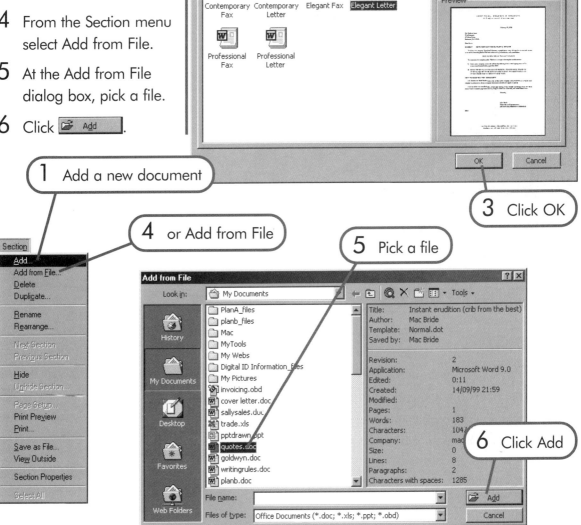

2 Pick a template

1 Add a new document

3 Click OK

4 or Add from File

5 Pick a file

6 Click Add

Sections and files

If you have a number of files that you want to pull into a binder, it may be quicker to drag them in from their Explorer folder.

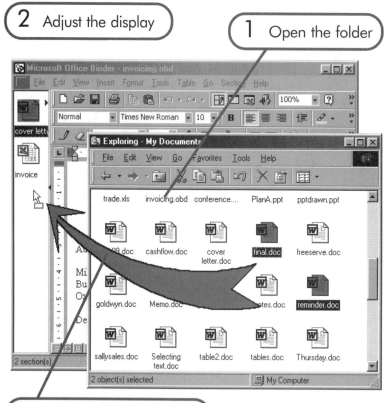

2 Adjust the display

1 Open the folder

3 Drag into the section list

Saving sections

Whether the sections were created within the binder, or brought in from file, once in place they form into a single structure – a binder document is saved as one file. However, it is possible to save a section as a separate file if required.

❑ Dragging files

1 Run Explorer or My Computer and open the file's folder.

2 Adjust the display so that the Binder section pane is in view.

3 Drag the file into the Binder, dropping it into place in the list.

❑ Saving sections

4 Switch to the section.

5 From the Section menu select Save as File.

6 Complete the Save dialog box as normal.

5 Use Section –
Save as File

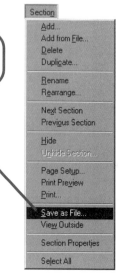

Basic steps

Duplicating sections

1 Switch to the source document.

2 From the Section menu, select Duplicate.

3 Choose where the new document is to fit.

4 Click [OK].

5 Click in the duplicate's name and edit it.

One of the useful features of binders is that you can easily duplicate a section. For instance, if you wanted several Word documents, all with the same letterhead, you could design the first, then duplicate that document to give you a basis for the others.

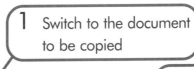

1 Switch to the document to be copied

2 Use Section – Duplicate

5 Edit the name

3 Insert after which?

4 Click OK

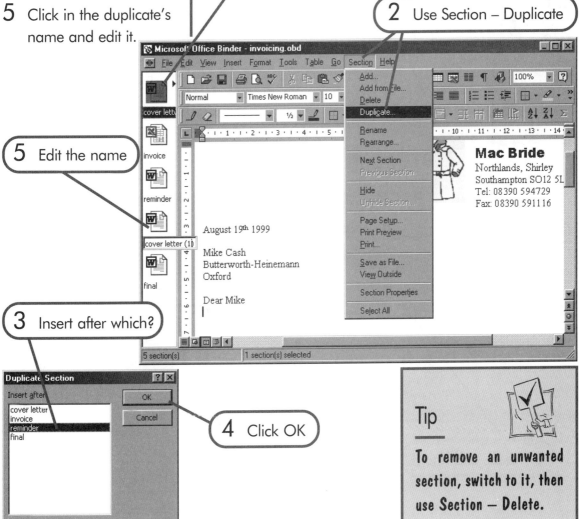

Tip

To remove an unwanted section, switch to it, then use Section – Delete.

Multiple views

An apparent drawback to the binder is that it can only display one section at a time. There is a simple way round this. The View Outside facility lets you open a free-standing copy of the application to handle a section.

Basic steps

1 Switch to the section you want to view.

2 From the Section menu select View Outside.

3 Back in the Binder, open the other section.

4 Set the display so that you can flip between binder and application.

5 Use File – Close and Return to exit from the outside application.

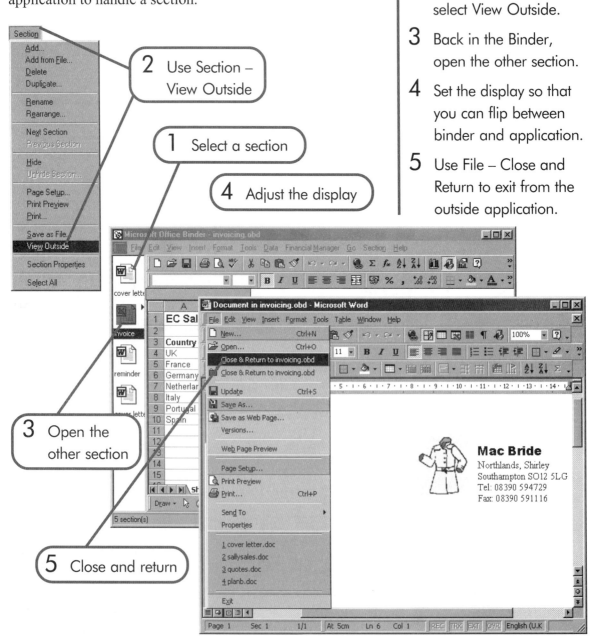

2 Use Section – View Outside

1 Select a section

4 Adjust the display

3 Open the other section

5 Close and return

Basic steps

Printing

1 Open the first section to be printed.

2 Hold [Ctrl] and click the other sections.

3 Open the File menu and select Print Binder.

4 Set the Print What option to All or Selected sections.

5 Set the Numbering to Continuous or Restart each section.

6 Click [OK].

You can print all the sections of the binder at once or select one or more for printing. If you are printing a selection, this must be set up first.

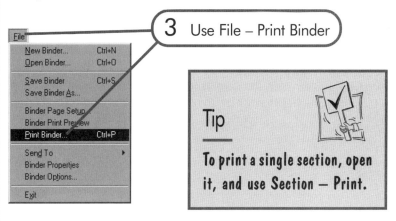

(3 Use File – Print Binder)

Tip

To print a single section, open it, and use Section – Print.

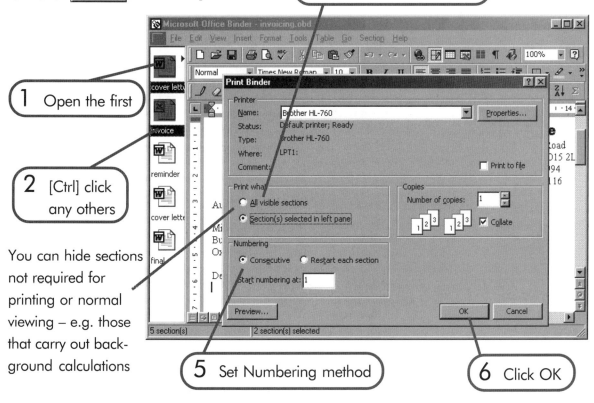

(4 Print All or a Selection)

(1 Open the first)

(2 [Ctrl] click any others)

You can hide sections not required for printing or normal viewing – e.g. those that carry out background calculations

(5 Set Numbering method)

(6 Click OK)

Summary

❑ A Binder holds a set of documents from the same or different applications.

❑ The documents in binders are referred to as sections.

❑ An empty Binder window is little more than a frame with a small section of commands for opening binders and adding sections.

❑ An application window, within a binder, has a Section menu and panel on the left side holding section icons.

❑ New binders are created by pulling in existing files or creating new documents from within the binder.

❑ Sections can be saved as separate files if needed.

❑ If you need to see more than one section at a time, the View Outside feature lets you open a separate copy of an application to edit a section.

❑ You can print the whole binder or one or more selected sections in one operation.

11 Outlook

Getting organised

Outlook is a personal organiser, and if you are on a local or extended network, it can also be used for arranging meetings of group members.

This is a multi-function system, with its various parts accessed through the **Outlook Bar** down the left side. When you select an item from here, it is displayed in the main window.

The bar has three groups.

Outlook Shortcuts

- **Outlook Today**, a summary of your appointments, current tasks and e-mail waiting for processing;

- **Inbox**, containing you new mail messages – and old ones that have not yet been deleted or filed elsewhere!

- A **Calendar**, with a reminder facility (page 178);

- A list of **Contact** names, addresses, phone and fax numbers, with a built-in phone dialler (page 176);

- A **Tasks** list, for scheduling tasks and monitoring their progress (page 184);

- **Notes** for jotting down reminders to yourself – these can be stuck anywhere on the desktop.

The elements can be interrelated, linking tasks to contacts or meetings, and contacts to meetings.

My Shortcuts

These links are to the less-used folders and facilities:

- **Drafts**, where messages can be held before completion;

- **Outbox**, where message sit while waiting for delivery;

- **Sent**, where copies of your messages are kept;

The display varies with the element being used, and has special options for each type. This screenshot is from Calendar in a Week view, set here to show a 7-day diary, the month and the Task list.

- **Outlook Update**, which links to Microsoft's on-line update service;

- **Journal** for logging activites (page 186);

Other Shortcuts

These provides access to regularly-used folders. You will find links to *My Computer*, and to the *My Documents* and *Favorites* folders. Files can be managed here, just as in Explorer – use it to open, view, print, rename, or send them to another disk or through the mail. You can even run programs from here!

Click to open the function

This deletes any selected item

Display options

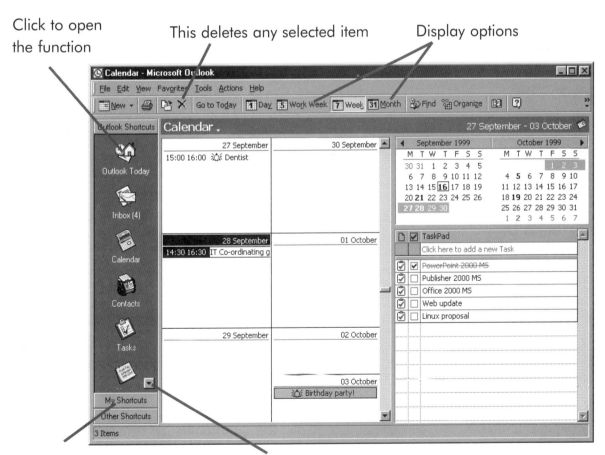

Click to open up the group   Scroll to reach other items in the group

The Contacts list

This is probably the most straightforward part of Outlook to set up. Mind you, it will take a while if you give all the details that it can hold – home and business address, phone and fax, birthdays, spouse, assistant, dog's name…

Basic steps

1 Open Contacts.

2 Open the New menu and select Contact or click ⬚ New .

3 On the General tab, enter the name and other contact details.

4 Switch to other tabs to add more if wanted.

5 Click 🖫 Save and Close .

❑ The new name will be slotted into the list in alphabetical order

1 Open Contacts

2 Use New – Contact

5 Save and Close

4 Any other details?

3 Enter details

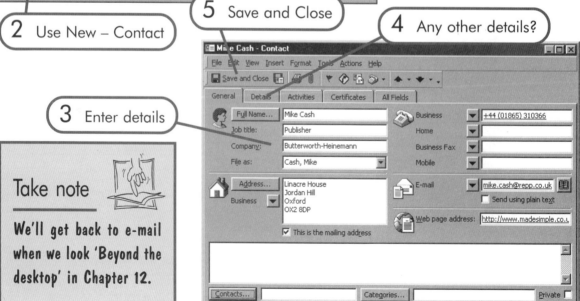

Take note

We'll get back to e-mail when we look 'Beyond the desktop' in Chapter 12.

Basic steps

1 Open Contacts.

2 Use the index buttons, if necessary, to get to the right place.

3 Select the person.

4 Click ⌨ or select Call Contact from the Actions menu.

5 Click Start Call.

6 Lift the phone.

7 When you want to hang up, click End Call.

Phone dialling

If your phone is connected through the PC's modem, you can get Outlook to dial for you.

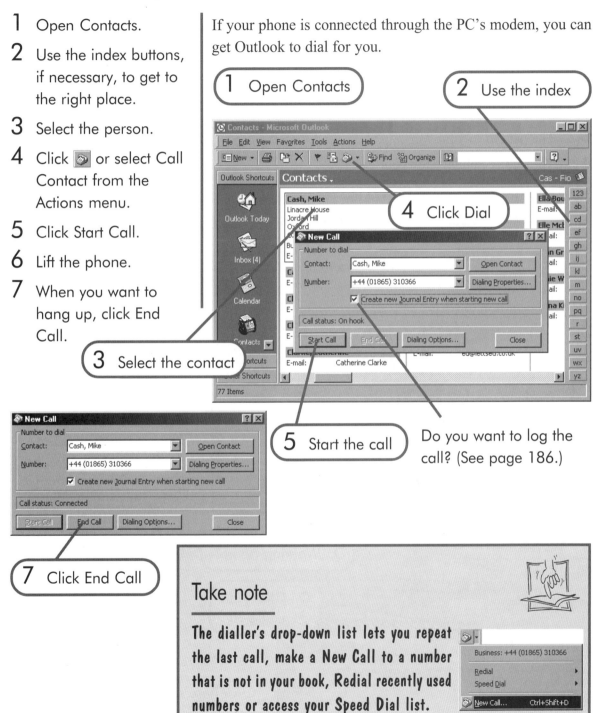

1 Open Contacts

2 Use the index

4 Click Dial

3 Select the contact

5 Start the call

Do you want to log the call? (See page 186.)

7 Click End Call

Take note

The dialler's drop-down list lets you repeat the last call, make a New Call to a number that is not in your book, Redial recently used numbers or access your Speed Dial list.

Calendar options

Many of the Outlook options can be left at their defaults; some should be looked at when you have got used to Outlook and want to fine-tune it; the Calendar needs early attention. You need to set the defaults for:

● How long before a meeting you receive a reminder;

● The pattern of your working week, and working day;

● The public holidays for your country.

Basic steps

1 Open Tools menu and select Options...

2 On the Preferences tab, set length of the Reminder notice.

3 Click Calendar Options... .

4 Tick your working days.

5 Set your normal working hours.

6 Click Add Holidays... .

7 Select the countries.

8 Click OK then close the Options window.

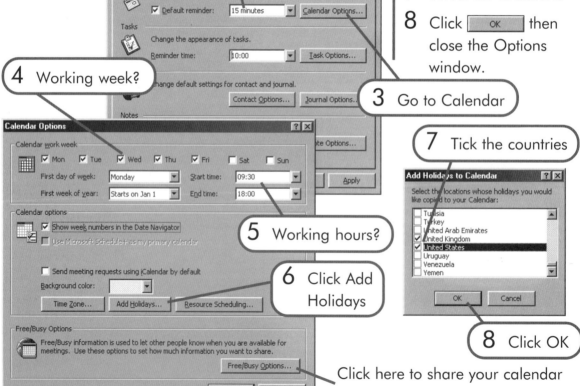

2 Set the Reminder notice

4 Working week?

3 Go to Calendar

5 Working hours?

6 Click Add Holidays

7 Tick the countries

8 Click OK

Click here to share your calendar bookings with networked colleagues

Basic steps

1 Open the Calendar.

2 Switch to 1 Day view.

3 Select the day.

4 Point to the start time and drag highlight to the planned end time.

5 Click ⊞ New or select Appointment from the New menu.

6 Enter a Subject.

7 Enter the Location.

8 Click 🖫 Save and Close.

Making a date

A simple appointment can be set up in seconds.

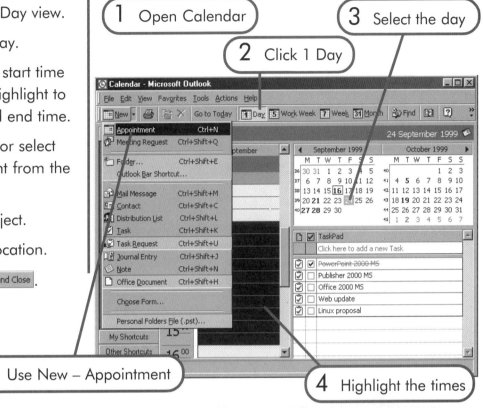

1 Open Calendar

2 Click 1 Day

3 Select the day

5 Use New – Appointment

4 Highlight the times

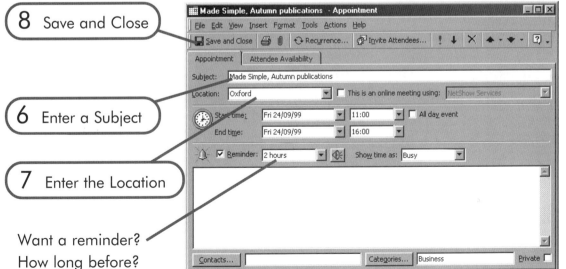

8 Save and Close

6 Enter a Subject

7 Enter the Location

Want a reminder? How long before?

Recurring appointments

If you have a series of regular appointments, you can set them all up in one operation.

1 Set up the first date

2 Click Recurrence

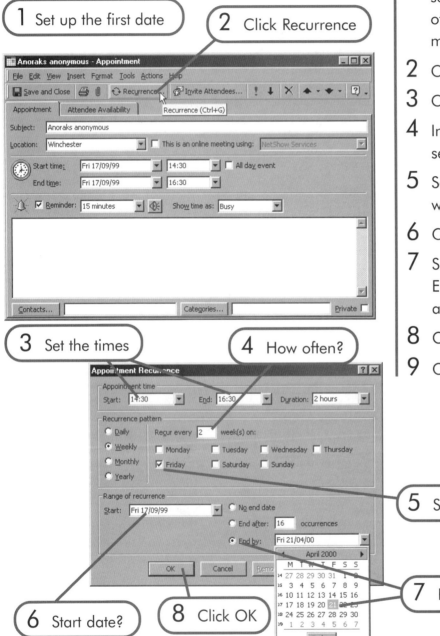

3 Set the times

4 How often?

5 Set the day

6 Start date?

7 End date?

8 Click OK

Basic steps

1 Follow steps 1 to 7 on the previous page to set the day and time of the first appoint-ment of the series.

2 Click ↻ Recurrence... .

3 Check the times.

4 In Recurrence pattern, set the frequency.

5 Set the Day (of the week, month or year).

6 Check the Start date.

7 Select No end date, or End after or End by and set the limit.

8 Click [OK] .

9 Click 🖫 Save and Close .

Arranging meetings

1 Select the day and time as for an appointment (see page 179).

2 Select New – Meeting Request from the Calendar menu.

3 Click the To: button.

...cont

This is probably of most use to people working on a local area network, where each has access to the (public) diary of the others. But, it is also a convenient way to call a meeting with those whom you can contact by fax or e-mail.

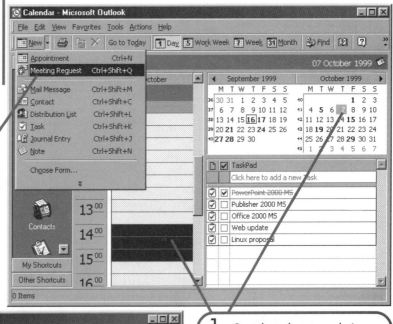

2 Use New – Meeting Request

3 Click To:

1 Set the date and time

Take note

When you have finished arranging the meeting, Outlook will send faxes and e-mails containing the details and notes you have typed into the Appointment panel.

4 Select the source for the names

5 Select and copy across

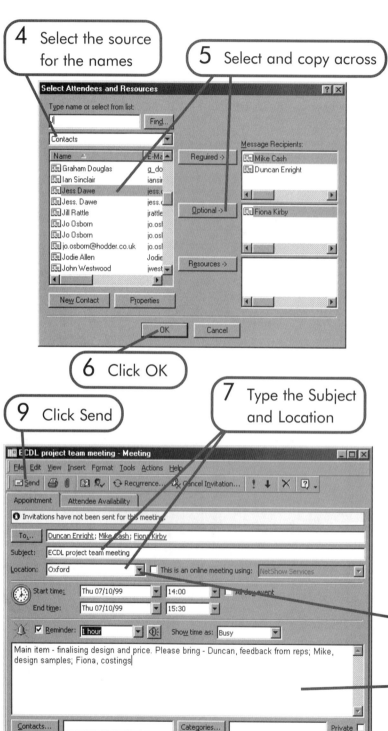

6 Click OK

9 Click Send

7 Type the Subject and Location

8 Add a message

4 Select the source for the names – probably Post Office Address book for the local area network and Contacts for external mail and fax.

5 Select the attendees who are Required or Optional, or will supply Resources, and click the buttons to copy them to the appropriate panes.

6 Click ⬚ OK ⬚.

7 Back at the Appointment panel, type the Subject and Location.

8 Type any message that you want to add to the meeting notice.

9 Click Send.

Previously-used locations can be picked from the drop-down list

Basic steps

1 If you have closed the Appointment window, double-click on the time to re-open it.

2 Switch to the Attendee Availability tab.

3 Check for clashes – you can only do this for people on your local network.

❑ To adjust the time

4 Drag the start or end line for minor adjustments.

Or

5 Click ⟨⟨ | AutoPick ▼ | ⟩⟩ heading backwards and forwards to let Outlook find the next free time for all attendees.

6 Type a message on the Appointments panel, if needed.

7 Click Send, or if you have already sent a request, click Send Update.

Checking availability

Where the other attendees are on your local area network – and are all using Outlook's Calendar to plan their time – you can check their availability. On the Attendee Availability tab, you can see who is busy when, and can rearrange your meeting time if necessary.

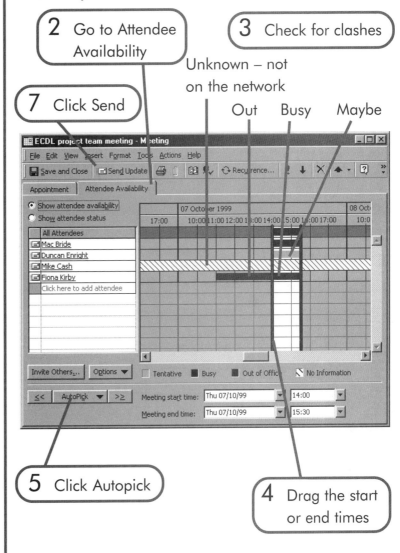

2 Go to Attendee Availability

3 Check for clashes

Unknown – not on the network

Out   Busy   Maybe

7 Click Send

5 Click Autopick

4 Drag the start or end times

Tasks

Use the Tasks module to keep track of your current and scheduled tasks. For each task you can record:

● The start and due dates;

● The percentage complete;

● The status and priority;

● The *Categories* – this can be just a way of keeping the same kinds of jobs together, or it can be a way of organising multi-part projects and monitoring the progress of the component tasks.

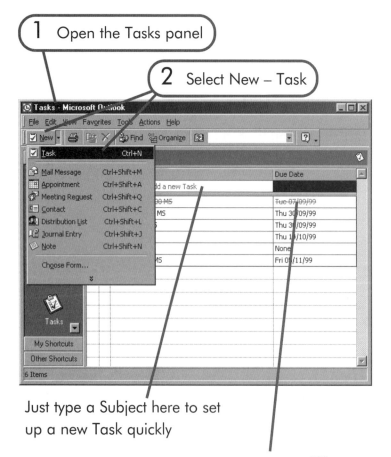

1 Open the Tasks panel

2 Select New – Task

Just type a Subject here to set up a new Task quickly

Completed tasks are crossed off – use ✖ to delete them when the records are no longer needed

1 Open the Tasks panel.

2 Drop down the New list and select Task or click ☑ New .

3 Type a Subject.

4 Set the Due date and Start date, if relevant.

5 Select the Status from the drop-down list.

6 Click Categories... .

7 Select one or more Categories.

8 Click OK .

9 Switch to the Details tab and add any known details.

10 Click 🖫 Save and Close .

Take note

If you don't want to enter the details for a new task, type the Subject into the 'Click here to add a new task' slot. Double-click to open the Task panel, and add or edit the details later.

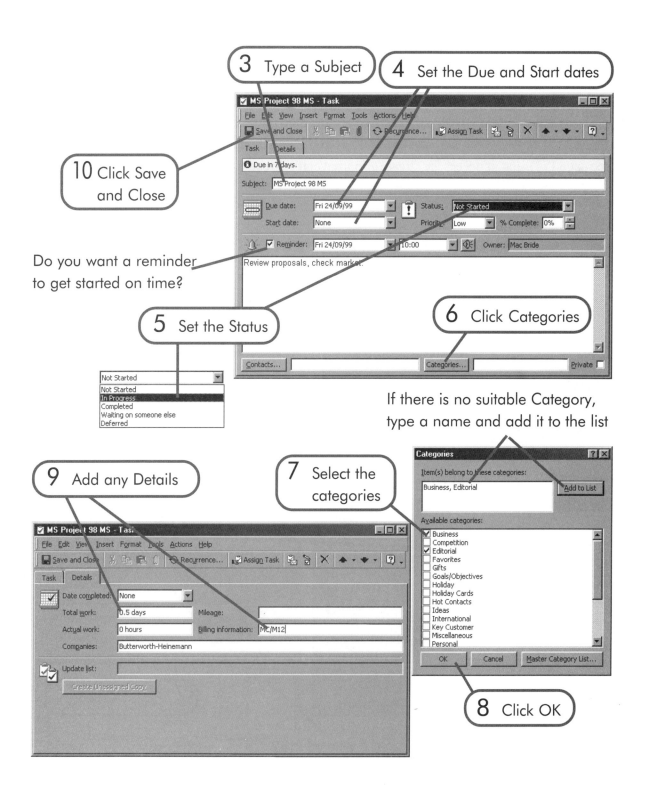

3 Type a Subject

4 Set the Due and Start dates

10 Click Save and Close

Do you want a reminder to get started on time?

5 Set the Status

6 Click Categories

If there is no suitable Category, type a name and add it to the list

9 Add any Details

7 Select the categories

8 Click OK

185

Logging activities

If you need to keep a record of work done – either for your own later reference, or for billing purposes – it can be logged in the Journal. The simplest way to do this is to get Outlook to log the activities that you normally need to record – unwanted entries are easily removed. You can also log calls as you make them (see page 177), and, if necessary, create a Journal entry directly.

(see page 177)

Basic steps

1 Open the Tools menu and select Options.

2 Click `Journal Options...`.

3 Tick the items, files and contacts you want to log and click OK.

❑ Single entry

4 Open the Journal panel and click `New`.

5 Type the Subject.

6 Note the time spent.

7 Select a Category.

8 Click `Save and Close`.

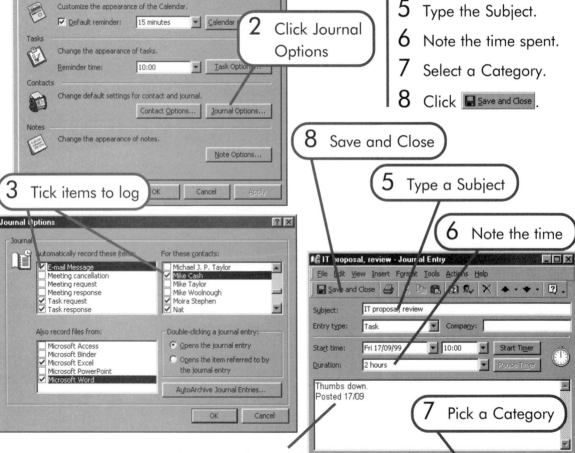

2 Click Journal Options

8 Save and Close

5 Type a Subject

6 Note the time

3 Tick items to log

7 Pick a Category

Add a note if wanted

186

Basic steps

- ❏ Using the Journal
- 1 Open the Journal.
- 2 Select a View – the *Last Seven Days* view is probably the best.
- 3 Right-click on an entry for the short menu.
- 4 Select Open Journal Entry to edit the entry.
- 5 Select Open Item Referred To to open logged files in their applications.
- ❏ Contact Activities
- 6 Go to Contacts and select the person.
- 7 Switch to the Activities tab.
- 8 Select the type of items from the Show list.

Viewing activities

If you want to view all your logged activities, the Journal panel is the place to do it. However, it may often be more useful to view the activities in relation to a contact, and this is best done through the Contacts panel.

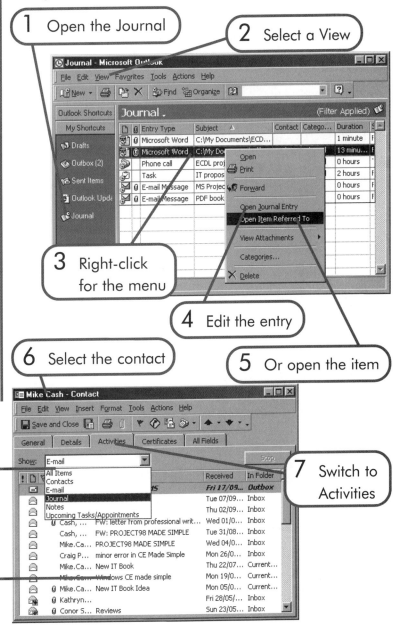

1 Open the Journal

2 Select a View

3 Right-click for the menu

4 Edit the entry

6 Select the contact

5 Or open the item

8 Select the items to show

7 Switch to Activities

All relevant items are listed, not just the logged ones – to see just those, select Journal in the Show list

Notes

If you are the sort of person who writes notes to yourself, here is an alternative to having Post-Its™ stuck to the side of your monitor. Outlook Notes save paper, and they don't drop off! You can keep them in the Notes folder, or stick them anywhere on your desktop – though not onto documents.

Basic steps

1 Open the Notes panel.

2 Open the New menu and select Note or click 📝 New.

3 Type your note – if you put a title in the top line, it will stand out more in the folder.

4 Drag the note onto the desktop, if wanted.

5 Click ❌ to close the note – it will be saved.

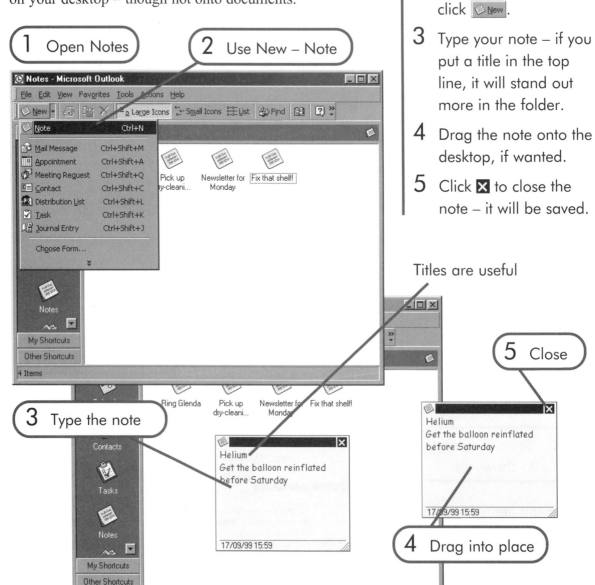

Reminders

We have seen that you can set reminders for appointments and tasks. Those for appointments appear 15 minutes (or however long you chose) before the event; reminders for tasks appear at a set time (normally the start) of the day.

If Office Assistant is running, it gives the reminder; if not, a standard message box is used. The options are the same either way.

● Click **Dismiss** to clear the reminder;

● Set the delay and click **Snooze** (or **Remind me again**) for a further reminder;

● Use **Open Item** to read the event or task panel.

OK, I'll get my coat

What am I supposed to be doing?

This job is running late – give me a few more days!

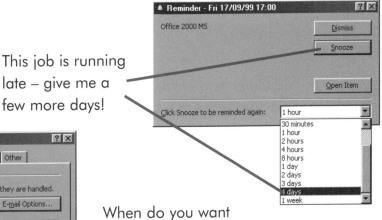

When do you want Task reminders?

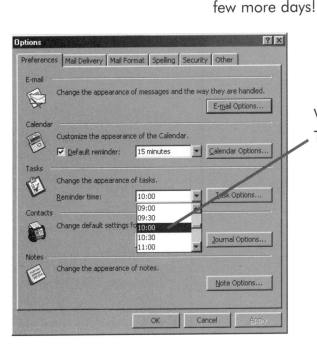

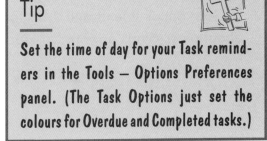

Tip

Set the time of day for your Task reminders in the Tools – Options Preferences panel. (The Task Options just set the colours for Overdue and Completed tasks.)

Summary

- ❑ Outlook is a personal and workgroup organiser in which you can store contacts, appointments and lists of tasks.

- ❑ The Contacts list can be used to record very complete details of your contacts.

- ❑ You can dial phone numbers in your Contacts list by clicking the dialler button.

- ❑ Most of the Options can be left at their defaults, but you should set up the Calendar options, and the Reminder notice time.

- ❑ When adding appointments, you can set them to recur weekly, monthly or at any fixed interval.

- ❑ Reminders can be set for any time before an appointment.

- ❑ You can use Outlook to arrange meetings with other users on your local area network, or who are accessible by e-mail or fax.

- ❑ The Task list can be used to schedule activities and to record progress on them. Reminders can be set for time-limited tasks.

- ❑ The Journal can log your activities automatically, and entries can also be made at any time.

- ❑ You need never forget anything if you set Reminders for your appointments and tasks, and stick Notes about other things on your Desktop.

Take note

The Mail-handling aspects of Outlook are covered in Chapter 12, Beyond the desktop.

12 Beyond the desktop

Internet links

In the Microsoft vision of the future, the world is your desktop. They see a time when the Internet will be as accessible as your local area network, and you will exchange ideas and documents as easily with colleagues around the world as you do now with those in your office.

In Windows 98, *Windows Explorer* and *Internet Explorer* are fully interchangeable. They may look different when you first run them, but that is only because of the way you have used them – open the Folders in Internet Explorer's sidebar, and it turns into Windows Explorer; type an Internet URL into the address line of Windows Explorer and it turns into Internet Explorer! You can use either to access the files on your hard disks, the other computers on your local network, the pages of the World Wide Web and everything else that is on-line.

Office 2000 takes a big step along that same road, with Web browsing and e-mail facilities in all its applications, and links to Internet resources at key points (see opposite).

The Web toolbar will be familiar to anyone who has used Internet Explorer.

Tip

If you have Internet Explorer or any other Web browser on your system, this will be activated when you try to go anywhere using the Web toolbar in an Office application. You can stop this by going to Windows Explorer and removing or redefining the HTM and HTML File Types. I wouldn't bother. The browser will load up in a few seconds, and it will do a better job than the application.

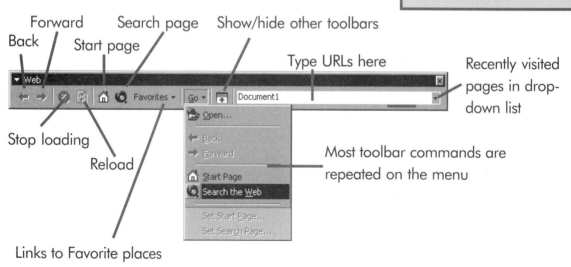

Back
Forward
Start page
Search page
Show/hide other toolbars
Type URLs here
Recently visited pages in drop-down list
Stop loading
Reload
Links to Favorite places
Most toolbar commands are repeated on the menu

The Clip Gallery offers a good example of the 'world-is-your-desktop' approach – and of its limitations.

A quick click on 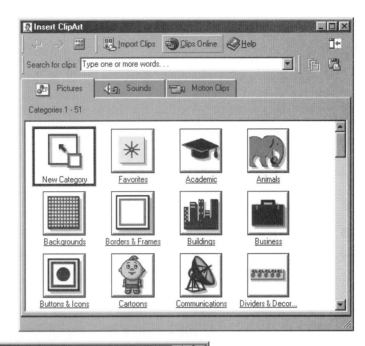 should take you to Microsoft's Clip Gallery on the Web. If you have a fast ISDN connection to the Internet, you will get there quickly. If the Microsoft site, and the main Internet connections, are not too busy, you will be able to find and download files quickly...

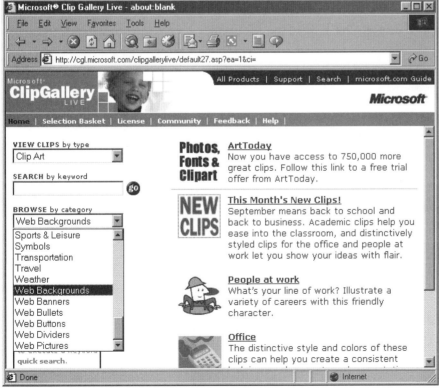

...but if you have a dial-up connection, and the site or the Internet's lines are busy, you will wait ages for your files. It will take a lot more development of the world's telephone connections, and of the Internet's hardware before we will all be able to treat the Internet as a simple extension of our desktops.

Outlook Inbox

Outlook's mail system is organised through four folders:

● **Inbox**, where incoming mail is stored. Messages remain in here until you delete them or move them elsewhere.

● **Drafts**, where part-written messages can be saved. Use the File – Save command while working on a message, and it will be saved in this folder. You can later reopen it, finish it and send as normal.

● **Outbox**, where messages sit while awaiting delivery;

● **Sent Items**, which stores copies of all outgoing mail. If not wanted, you can turn off the automatic copying in the E-mail options of the Tools – Options – Preferences panel.

The Inbox is the one you will use most often, and is located in the Outlook shortcuts. If you are on a local area network with a permanent connection to the Internet, all your new mail will probably be sent directly to it. If not, you'll have to pick up the mail for yourself.

❏ Getting the mail

1 Click  Send/Receive or open the Tools menu, point to Send/Receive and select your mail service.

2 If you are not on-line, Outlook will start up the connection. Wait while it connects.

3 Tick Hang up when finished unless you want to go surfing afterwards.

Tip

You can create new folders for long-term organised storage, if required. Use File – New – Folder, and copy or move items just as in Windows Explorer.

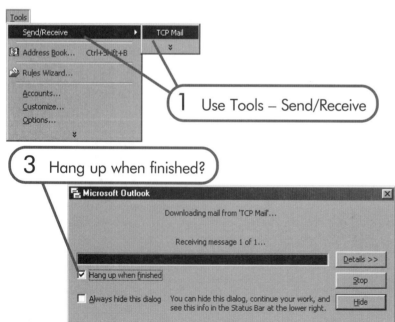

1 Use Tools – Send/Receive

3 Hang up when finished?

Basic steps

❏ Reading and replying

1 Click on a message, or right-click and select Open.

2 Read the message.

3 Use the buttons or the Actions menu, and select Reply, or Reply to All (send to all who received a copy), or Forward (send a copy to another person).

4 Select Plain Text or HTML format.

5 Continue as for sending mail (next page).

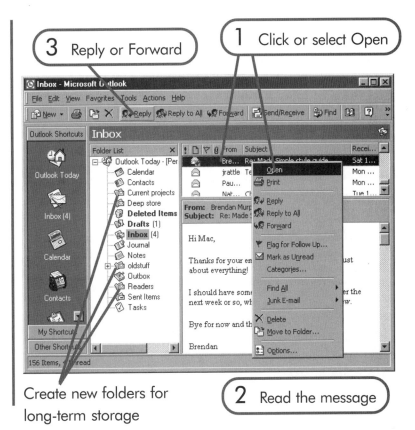

3 Reply or Forward

1 Click or select Open

2 Read the message

Create new folders for long-term storage

4 Plain Text or HTML?

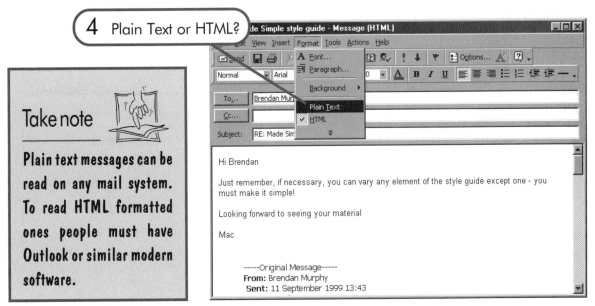

Take note

Plain text messages can be read on any mail system. To read HTML formatted ones people must have Outlook or similar modern software.

195

Sending e-mail

E-mail has transformed business and personal communications. It is cheap, fast and reliable – and if a message does not get through, your mail server will let you know. But it does need to be used with a bit of thought.

● Type a clear **Subject** line, so your recipients know that your message is not junk e-mail to be ignored;

● Keep messages short – people may have to pay for phone time to download them.

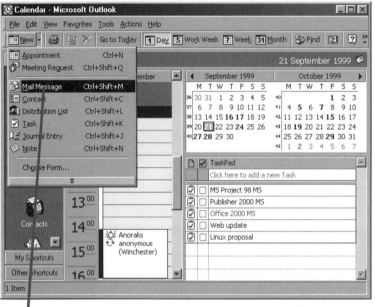

1 Use New – Mail Message

You can start a new message from any part of Outlook.

Basic steps

1 In any part of Outlook select Mail Message from the New... menu.

Or   .

2 In Inbox or any mail folder, click 🖹 New .

3 At the new message window, click To... .

4 Select the recipient and click To -> or Cc -> for copies – repeat if needed.

5 Click OK .

6 Type a Subject, then your message.

7 Click 🖪 Options... to open the Options panel.

8 Set the Sensitivity, Delivery time and other options as required and click Close.

9 Click Send.

Take note

If an address is not in your Contacts, you can add it at step 4.

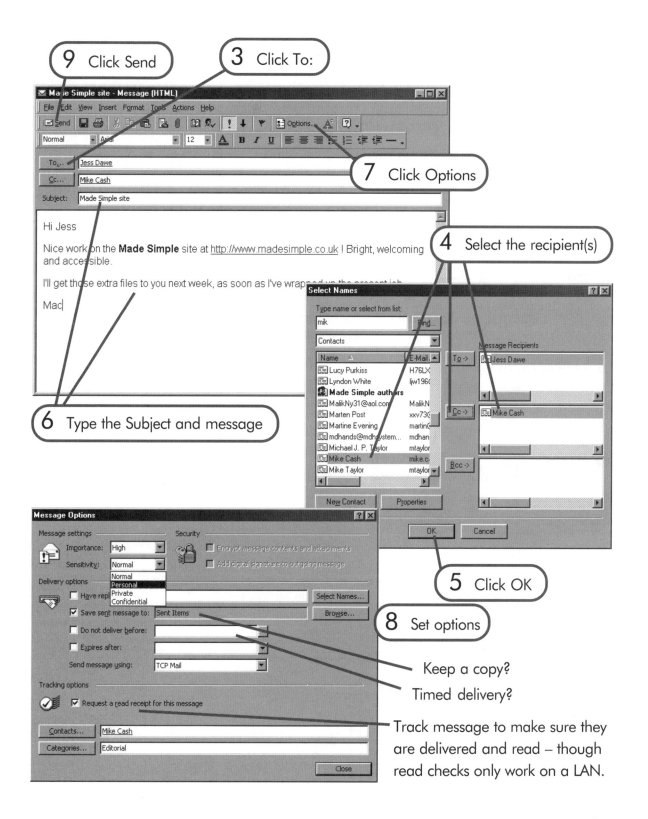

9 Click Send

3 Click To:

7 Click Options

4 Select the recipient(s)

6 Type the Subject and message

5 Click OK

8 Set options

Keep a copy?

Timed delivery?

Track message to make sure they are delivered and read – though read checks only work on a LAN.

Files by wire

Experts have been telling us for years that computers will create the paperless office, but in most offices so far they seem to have created even more paper. Office can help to reverse that!

- Send e-mail documents, from within an application.
- Attach documents to e-mail messages as you write them.
- Circulate documents, by adding a Routing slip.
- Send faxes directly from your PC, without printing first.

Basic steps

- ❑ E-mailing documents
- 1 From the File menu, select Send To then Mail Recipient (as Attachment)...
- ❑ The new message window opens, with the document embedded in the message area.
- 2 Click **To...** and select the recipient(s).
- 3 If the document has been given a Title, it will be copied into the Subject line – if not, type a header here.
- 4 Add a message and send as usual.

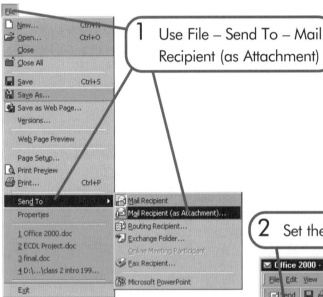

1 Use File – Send To – Mail Recipient (as Attachment)

2 Set the recipient

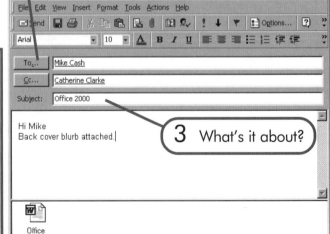

3 What's it about?

Tip

Send To – Mail Recipient converts Word into an e-mail system so that you can send the document as a message. Click 🔲 on the standard Toolbar to revert to the normal Word screen.

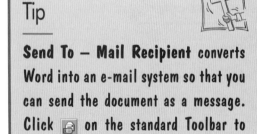

Basic steps

Routing slips

1 From the File menu, select Send To then Routing Recipient...

2 Click **Address...** and select the recipients.

3 Click **Route** to circulate the document immediately.

or

4 Click **Add Slip** to leave it set for later routing.

If you want several people to see and make comments on a draft document, you can circulate it around the internal network, or through your Internet connections, by adding a Routing slip. You can control the order in which the document is circulated, and also what can be done to it.

● Use **Tracked changes** to turn on revision marking, so that you can see what changes have been made;

● Use **Comments**, to allow others to add notes, but not change the document;

● The **Forms** option is only for circulating forms for collecting information.

Tip

To Learn more about using Outlook, see *Outlook 2000 Made Simple.*

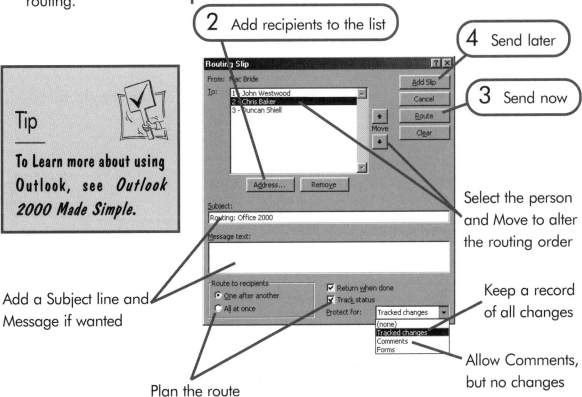

2 Add recipients to the list

4 Send later

3 Send now

Select the person and Move to alter the routing order

Add a Subject line and Message if wanted

Keep a record of all changes

Plan the route

Allow Comments, but no changes

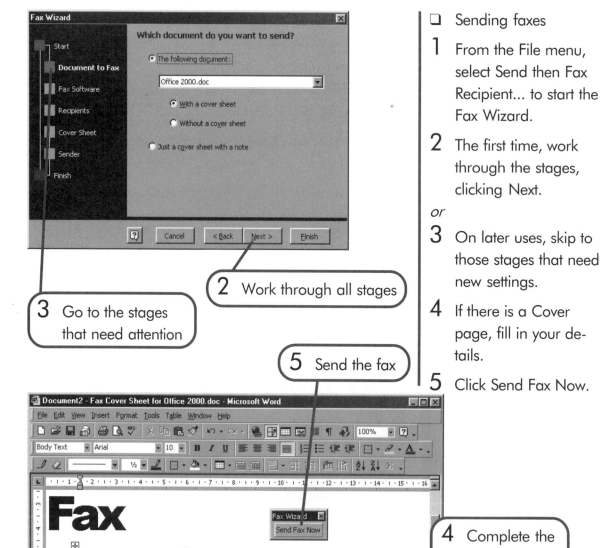

2 Work through all stages

3 Go to the stages
that need attention

5 Send the fax

4 Complete the
cover sheet

Double-click on
check boxes to tick
(or clear) them

❏ Sending faxes

1 From the File menu,
select Send then Fax
Recipient... to start the
Fax Wizard.

2 The first time, work
through the stages,
clicking Next.

or

3 On later uses, skip to
those stages that need
new settings.

4 If there is a Cover
page, fill in your de-
tails.

5 Click Send Fax Now.

Basic steps

- ❏ Attaching files

1 Start to write a new message .

2 Open the Insert menu, select File or click 📎.

3 Type the Filename or browse for the file.

4 Click Insert ▾.

5 Complete and send the message as usual.

Tip

Sometimes a hyperlink will do the job better than inserting the file. See the next page.

Attached files

Any files – from any application, not just Office 2000 – can be attached or linked to an e-mail. Use a Link if the recipient is on your local network, and the document file is in a public folder – it is more efficient that actually sending the file.

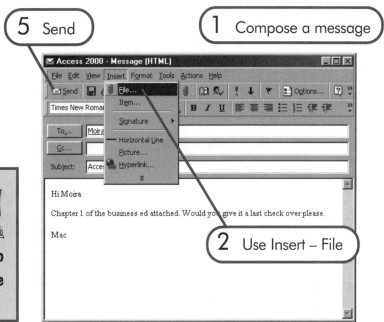

5 Send

1 Compose a message

2 Use Insert – File

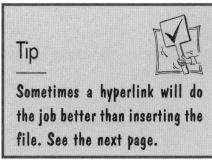

3 Select the file

4 Click Insert

Text files can be inserted into the body of the message

Same effect as clicking the Insert button

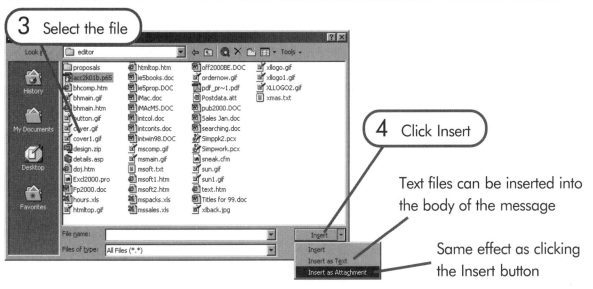

Hyperlinks

A hyperlink can take you from one file to another on the same computer or on a totally different system on the other side of the world. All Office 2000 applications can handle hyperlinks. You can create them and travel along them in e-mail messages, Word reports, spreadsheets or databases.

If your document is going to be read by other Office 2000 users, and you want to draw their attention to a file on a public folder in your computer or network, or on the Internet, don't embed it or attach it – use a hyperlink.

Basic steps

❏ Creating a hyperlink

1 Select the word or phrase (or picture).

2 Use Insert – Hyperlink or click 🖳.

3 Type or select the Internet address or the file to be linked.

4 Click [OK].

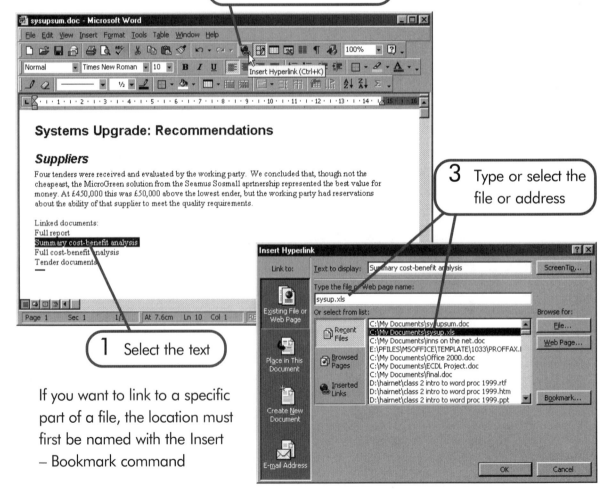

2 Click Insert Hyperlink

3 Type or select the file or address

1 Select the text

If you want to link to a specific part of a file, the location must first be named with the Insert – Bookmark command

Basic steps

❑ Using hyperlinks

1 Click on the underlined word or phrase.

2 Wait for the linked document (and its application) to load.

3 The Web toolbar will have appeared. Use its Back and Forwards buttons to navigate between the linked documents.

If you pause over a link, the hand pointer appears and the address of the file or Web page is shown

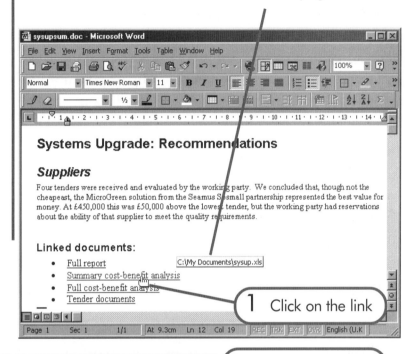

3 Move between the linked files

1 Click on the link

2 Wait while it loads

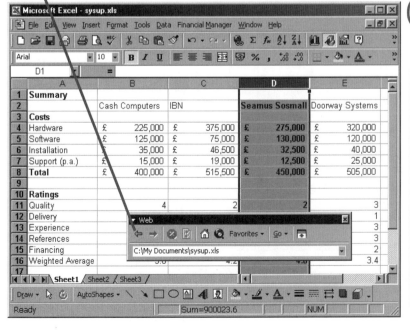

Tip

If you want to create a Web site, FrontPage 2000 is an ideal tool for the job. Read *FrontPage 2000 Made Simple* to find out more about it.

HTML

All Office 2000 documents can be saved in Web page (.HTM) format. This doesn't mean that you can save a file as HTM in one application and open it in another. That doesn't work – try to open an Excel-created Web page from within Word, and Excel will start up to open it. What it does mean is that the same documents can be printed out, used directly on your desktop machine and made available to others via the Internet or your organisation's intranet *without any extra work*!

That brochure you produced in Word can be printed for use in the showroom or put on the Web for on-line customers. Your PowerPoint presentation will become a set of linked Web pages. These are good, but there's better! With Excel – and Access if you have it – you can publish interactive pages. Visitors will be able to enter their own information and have it processed and the results displayed from the page. Here's how to create an Excel page with added interactivity.

Basic steps

1 Create the Excel spreadsheet. Unlock the cells where visitors can enter data, then turn on protection for the sheet to lock the rest. Save the sheet as normal, as a backup.

2 Select the active area.

3 Open the File menu and select Save As…

4 In the Save as type box, select *Web page*.

5 Set the *Selection* as the Save option.

6 Tick Add interactivity.

7 Click [Change Title…] and enter a title to go on the page, if wanted.

8 Enter the Filename.

9 Click [Publish…] to send the page directly to your Web server.

Or

10 Click [Save] to save it to file for publishing later.

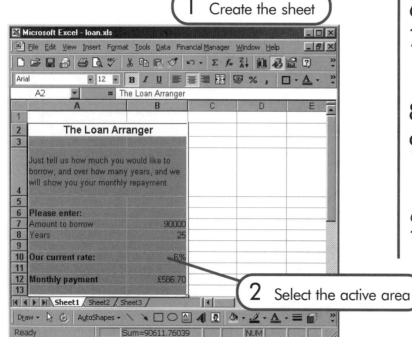

1 Create the sheet

2 Select the active area

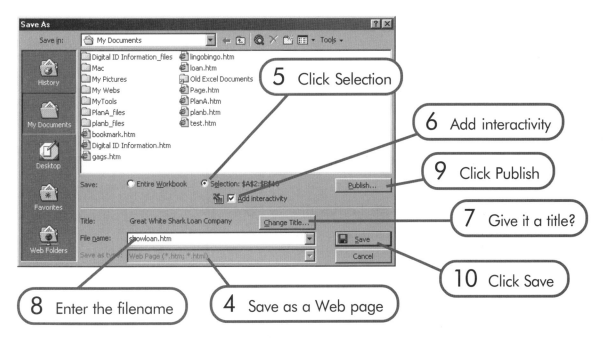

5 Click Selection

6 Add interactivity

9 Click Publish

7 Give it a title?

8 Enter the filename

4 Save as a Web page

10 Click Save

The page viewed in IE5 – the Monthly payment changes
when new values are entered for the Amount or Years

Take note

You can insert into documents, Web pages created in other applications, just as you can insert objects or copied blocks from them. The main advantage of inserted Web pages is that they can have the added interactivity.

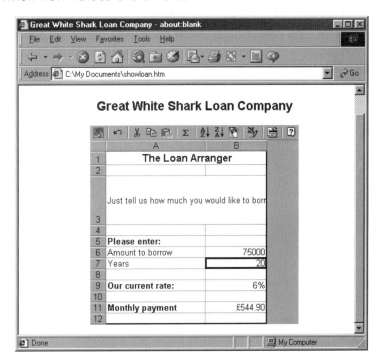

Summary

- ❏ Easy access to the Internet has been built into all the Office 2000 applications.

- ❏ Finding and downloading files from the Internet can take longer than you think!

- ❏ Use the Inbox to fetch and reply to your e-mail.

- ❏ When sending e-mail, do include a Subject line, and keep your messages brief.

- ❏ Documents can be sent by e-mail or fax directly from an Office 2000 application if you have a modem or are on a local area network.

- ❏ You can attach files from any application to an e-mail message.

- ❏ Hyperlinks can be used to link to files stored in public folders, or to Web pages and files on the Internet.

- ❏ Documents created in any Office application can be saved as Web pages. With Excel you can create inter-active pages.

Index